GLOBAL WAR

AN ATLAS OF WORLD STRATEGY

by EDGAR ANSEL MOWRER
and MARTHE RAJCHMAN

With an introduction by
The Honorable FRANK KNOX
Secretary of the Navy

NEW YORK : WILLIAM MORROW AND COMPANY : 1942

To
The uncounted other amateur strategists
of the United States

INTRODUCTION

By The Honorable FRANK KNOX, *Secretary of the Navy*

This is an ambitious atlas. To match its cheek, you would have to go back to the map-makers of early days, who painfully and ingeniously pieced together from direct experience, hearsay, legend and sheer imagination wonderful charts of strange regions, filling out the gaps with pictures of mermaids, fish, unicorns, gargoyles and inscriptions: *Hic Sunt Leones*—Here are Lions. The present authors have had to call upon their imagination to a degree hardly less. One of them, Edgar Ansel Mowrer, is a newspaper correspondent who for thirty years has been travelling about the planet and sticking his nose into unlikely parts of it at critical moments—notably during four wars; while the other, Miss Marthe Rajchman, is not only a skilled map-maker, author of several atlases, but a learned geographer from the Institut de Géographie at the University of Paris. As strategists, both are amateurs, writing and drawing for other amateurs.

Their chief problem was one of imaginative anticipation. How, in 120 pages of maps and texts, can you give the essentials for following the present conflict? Obviously there could be no question of portraying various fronts, with positions held by this army or by that, for these shift from day to day and from hour to hour. What the authors were seeking was an explanation that would remain good until the end of the coming peace conference. In other words, how best in a limited space illustrate and clarify this war not only in its past but in its coming phases, anticipating the sites of almost any battles and campaigns that could happen between existing states at the present state of technological advance?

In such a changing world, an attempt like this is decidedly an experiment. Even if it turns out that this is less a definitive answer to the problem than an invitation to others to undertake the same job, there remains the glory of exploration. And in the meantime, this atlas will have been of real help in visualizing the path of victory.

CONTENTS

GLOBAL WAR IN THREE DIMENSIONS

"War," said Heraclitus, "is the mother of all things."

Slightly exaggerated, no doubt. But a fine thing to remember at the close of a period of fatuous pacifism in which persons who went about insisting that "war never settles anything" were all too rarely contradicted.

Since 1935 we have been painfully relearning that war can settle a lot. It always has. It has made and unmade kingdoms and empires; it has destroyed or established religions; it has brought this people to eternal fame and that one to quick obscurity; it has made human societies strong or weak, penniless or prosperous.

Even though it cannot rival peace in pure creativity, it can hammer home in short order lessons that apparently no amount of peace can instill into careless brains. The latest of these is that never again can nations like ours expect to carry on each its separate existence in even relative independence of what is happening elsewhere. No frontier can ever be held firmly enough to prevent fifty thousand enemy parachutists from wafting down five hundred or a thousand miles behind it, in the course of a single night. Therefore in the absence of international police no people can ever again feel safe against powerful, well-armed neighbors unless it is itself permanently mobilized, on the alert, and garrisoned up and down its entire length and breadth. We are learning all this today.

Yet there is worse. War is henceforth not only three-dimensional, it is global. Science has shrunk the planet down to where the war god can span it with his two arms.

This startling message is not exactly new. But few believed it or took it to heart. For that it was necessary that battleships should clash all over the Seven Seas, freighters should founder under torpedo blows from Zanzibar to Novaya Zemlya; that troops should be rushed from New York to Batavia, be shuttled back and forth between Tobruk and Australia; that officials should go on missions from Panama to Dutch Harbor by way of Halifax, Murmansk, Kuibyshev and Komsomolsk; that bombers should trace a permanent girdle around the earth. Now we know that peace is indivisible—as they used to say at Geneva. So is war.

Largely because National Sovereignty is still sovereign! Each contemporary State, like the Children of Israel before the coming of the kings, tries to do what is right in its own (not seldom) bleary eyes. Hundreds of millions sing "Peace on Earth, Good

Will to Men" at Christmas time. The rest of the year it is "My Country, Right or Wrong!" For Sovereignty acknowledges no God outside itself.

Actually, this is bombast. The real sovereignty of each State is strictly limited by that of other States. But sovereignty seeks to become in fact as absolute as it is in theory. Therefore the rule is that all States are either trying to extend their sovereignty; or, like little fishes that accompany whales, are seeking safety from a Sovereign Protector; or are endeavoring, by a mixture of humility and defiance, to maintain a precarious neutrality. In other words, each State must either seek to maintain and increase its power or give up the struggle from lack of size or spirit, and thenceforth exist on sufferance. In the long run, no mere defense of *status quo* ever succeeded—and less than ever under present conditions where the political area is the world.

This is nobody's fault. It is not the inherent iniquity of men but the fact nearly all of them seek power, that makes for politics and wars. Whether in the back of a Chicago saloon or in the Kremlin, all politics are power politics. States are merely the appropriate organs of politics at specific moments. Politics between States are international politics—neither more nor less admirable than politics in city wards.

It is the dim acknowledgment of this that has made people accept wars. By the same token, they are now seeking for international politics that same sort of legal backlog that has transformed local politics from a series of murderous brawls between armed factions into (generally) bloodless vote-counting. When this is done, there need no longer be wars.

I. SOME CHARACTERISTICS OF THE GREAT POWERS IN 1939

GEOGRAPHY

States make politics and politics make States. In the struggle of human societies for pelf or prestige, certain peoples, through superior luck or courage or acumen, have always managed to get a head-start and grow bigger than the others. By accretion, multiplication or immigration, they swell beyond their fellows, and become the Great Powers of the age. Always in the past, one of them has finally swallowed all the others and become supreme in its area.

Our area is the planet. Therefore our Great Powers boss the world. They win the wars (or lose them). They try to keep a line or two out wherever the fishing may be good. This they call protecting their "interests" (an indifferent label for profits, prestige or power). Sometimes their rivalries result in a temporarily beneficial Balance of Power, thanks to which little States manage to carry on.

A world without Great Powers is entirely thinkable and conceivably desirable. But once they exist, their history is world history. For they alone have what it takes —extensive territories, large populations, wealth more or less decently come by, plentiful raw materials, industrial skill, ready acceptance of combat and prowess in fighting.

The American Army War College has an elaborate table for attempting to evaluate the war strength of a nation. Geographical, political, economic, psychological and combat factors are melted down, analyzed and evaluated and out of the whole is drawn a "combat potential" both "current" and "long-range."

Some such procedure is obviously essential, but it remains more of an art than a science. Many of the elements are completely subjective in character, others are physical and objective. Morale wins battles: how much can it compensate for faulty organization, or deficient natural wealth, or the wrong kind of equipment, or outmoded conceptions of strategy, or badly trained forces?

Some religions heighten, others diminish war potential. Cromwell's Ironsides, who prayed before they fought, were terrible in battle. So were Mohammed's fanatics. But Brahmans tend to pacifism and non-resistance. Buddhists are pacifists in Burma (up to a point!); in Japan, jingoes. Why were Buchmanites generally "appeasers"?

In any case, here a great many of the War College items have been ignored and an effort has been made to direct the attention to visible and commensurable factors with no final summing up of relative combat potential. After all, that is being demonstrated in much more convincing fashion on five continents and seven seas!

Since change is continual, it has been convenient to take the Great Powers as they were back in the fatal Year of Grace, 1939, when war, already conceived as "total" by General Ludendorff, made "perpetual" by the fascists, became literally "global."

Seven nations were then in the "heavy-weight" class and liked to call themselves *World Powers*.

Politically, this was a slight exaggeration.

Geographically, it was entirely so. No nation, however quarrelsome, has ever been extended enough to mix in every international brawl, regardless of location.

A rough description of the seven Great Powers of 1939 would run somewhat as follows:

Only one Power had a window on every ocean, a port on every sea, a foot in nearly every important door and a finger in every pie: the *British Commonwealth of Nations*. In a geographical sense it was the only approach to a World Power—a fact intolerable to the Germans and Japanese.

There were a couple of Two-Ocean Powers (or Three-Ocean, counting the Arctic), facing two ways at once and shifting weight now in this direction, now in that: the *United States of America* and the *Union of Soviet Socialist Republics*.

There was one Far Eastern Empire, Japan, pacific in ocean but not in notion, uneasily harboring the appetite of a thirty-foot python in the body of a ten-foot king cobra, vulnerable but venomous.

France draped most of its well-situated, balanced Atlantic and Mediterranean Empire cohesively across Europe and Northern Africa; the remainder lay beyond the power of metropolitan defense; in time of war, Madagascar on the Indian Ocean and Indo-China overlooking the China Sea were sure goners.

Hitler's Third Reich was well on the way to swallowing the rest of Europe. Its central position and concentration made it well situated for attack. But its ports were cramped and it was handicapped by the lack of free access to any ocean.

Last and noisiest among Great Powers was Mediterranean Italy, owing its desert Empire less to inherent plug-ugliness than to the supineness of its competitors, its steadfastness in procreation and its stage-belligerence.

BRITISH COMMONWEALTH OF NATIONS

The British Commonwealth of Nations, until the Statute of Westminster (1931) called the British Empire, was the only one of its kind and the only true World Power. To describe its strange amalgam of mother country, independent commonwealths, crown colonies, mandated territories, protectorates, etc., would take too long. The dominant fact is, though the British held more territory than anyone else, the basis of their greatness was not primarily land or numbers—but trade and innumerable naval bases scattered all over the planet. Trade made for wealth; far-flung naval bases plus many ships (which other countries might have built but could not have used so well for lack of bases) for sea power. Wealth plus dominant sea power brought about rapid industrialization. As a result, the nineteenth century was predominantly British.

No other sea power was left on the planet. Systematically or by instinct (the point is a subject of controversy), Great Britain had just naturally acquired foreign places. Hundreds of them. The habit of acquisition started in the seventeenth, gathered momentum in the eighteenth (offset by the loss of the Thirteen American Colonies) and really got going in the nineteenth century, when over seventy areas were gathered to the Empire. In the course of this process, Spain, Portugal, Holland and France were beaten and reduced as naval Powers. A German bid for sea power was nipped off in 1914-1918.

At the beginning of the Second World War, Britain controlled the two openings from the North Sea into the Atlantic; the Mediterranean (at Gibraltar, Malta and Suez); the Iberian Peninsula (by an alliance with Portugal); the North American waters (by bases at Halifax, Bermuda, in the Bahamas and the Caribbean); the South Atlantic (by bases on the West African Coast and island holdings close to Africa). The White Ensign waved over the Cape of Good Hope and the Falkland Islands, thus controlling the passage through the Straits of Magellan and around Cape Horn. Britain dominated the Indian Ocean, with the Red Sea, the Persian Gulf and the Bay of Bengal; had a stranglehold on all the passages from the Indian Ocean to the Pacific; was master of the China Sea, and of most of the Central and South Pacific Ocean. As late as 1939, of all the vital strategic passages from ocean to ocean, only one, Panama, was not in British hands.

Such was the British Commonwealth of Nations. It was not an accident. British rule was mild and generally beneficial. Everywhere they went they took with them personal liberty and the reign of law. They protected the empires of otherwise helpless little people, the Dutch, the Belgians, the Danes and the Portuguese. The safety of the two Americas during the nineteenth century depended upon 3000 miles of tossing water, the balance of power in Europe and a predominant British fleet.

Nonetheless, British power was waning. The reasons were several: decline of imperial feeling at home; decline of sea power as against land power and air power; centrifugal forces within the white parts of the Commonwealth (Australia, Canada and, notably, South Africa); growing determination of subject peoples like the Indians to achieve self-government; the decline of Britain's ally, France, and the rapid rise of Germany, Soviet Russia and the United States. Against a vast one- or two-continent coalition, capable of striking many blows against British possessions in three or four places at once, the Commonwealth was painfully vulnerable.

UNITED STATES OF AMERICA

The United States of America was the only country in the world that in 1939-1940 presented a balanced harmony of potential land, sea and air power.

Its vast territory gave it a definitely continental war potential and outlook. Its bay windows on both oceans, numerous on the Atlantic side, fewer toward the Pacific, encouraged the habit of the sea. The East Coast particularly offers plentiful harbors and navigable rivers that fairly invite a sailor's life. At various moments of its national existence the continental or the maritime outlook prevailed. New England clippers outdid the British at their best. At the turn of the twentieth century, the American war fleet was second in the world. At such times there was national expansion. The habit was, however, to expand and acquire external responsibilities (Alaska, the Hawaiian Islands, the Philippines and Guam, a friendly protectorate over Cuba, the Panama Canal, leaseholds on nearby British bases, etc.), then to turn back to internal colonization, and neglect national defenses. Up until the outbreak of the second World War, the paradoxical Americans oscillated between adventure bordering on rashness and extreme provincialism masquerading as pacifism, patriotism or economic uplift. They cheerfully assumed the obligation to defend all of South America, and provided themselves with less than half the means to do it with.

The advent of the Air Age gave promise of reconciling the two tendencies. It was no accident that the Americans should have taken the leading rôle in transoceanic air service, nor that with this they should have awakened to the fact that distant, half-forgotten possessions like the Philippines were worth defending.

Only when they found themselves gradually being drawn into a war they had done nearly everything to avoid, did the Americans accept the idea of strategical, as opposed to economic or hedonistic, lines of communication. Until then they had considered strategy part of the curse of old Europe, with its "eternal wars." Holding the Panama Canal turned out to be essentially an air and naval problem, for in all probability the Canal could be defended against a powerful enemy only by counter-offensive. The same was even truer of the far Pacific Islands, Wake, Guam, the Philippines and Samoa.

If, suddenly, the Americans found themselves forced to do the giant's share of defending the Western Hemisphere against a world coalition, then control of Iceland, Greenland and conceivably the Atlantic islands, the Azores, Canaries, Cape Verdes, etc., might turn out to be essential. Loss of the Brazilian bulge could be fatal to holding the Panama Canal or keeping the Caribbean inviolate.

The essential American strategical problem turned out, upon examination, to be psychological. In last analysis, this country could best defend itself by attack. But the people were conditioned against such an "offensive mentality." Too often they confused offensive strategy with unprovoked aggression. They had—at least until the advent of air power—little planetary sense, the sort of thing that the British had acquired with their empire and the Germans through the amazing size of their ambitions. The Americans in 1939—though they did not know it—were being invited by history to become world-conscious, either as conquerors or as pioneers in world organization. The one thing they could not choose, and escape downfall, was further isolation, either national or hemispheric.

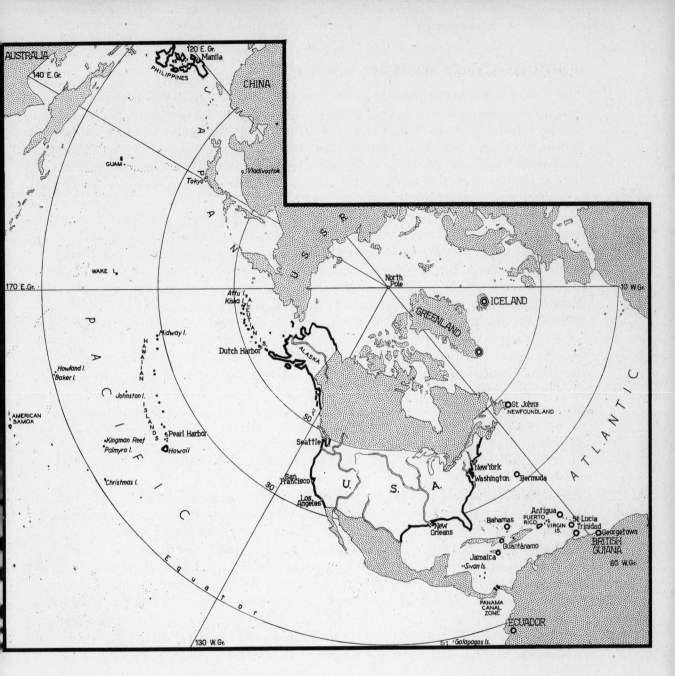

UNION OF SOVIET SOCIALIST REPUBLICS

The Union of Soviet Socialist Republics was the second largest empire and the biggest continuous country in the world. Its territories comprised an ungodly portion of the existing land, one-sixth according to Soviet authorities; one-seventh according to Junius Wood. Regardless of fractions, the Soviet territories measured something over six thousand miles from east to west, and nearly three thousand from north to south. Statistically, this colossus seemed overwhelming and would actually have been, were it not that many of its territories were unfit for habitation.

The reason is that they were too cold and too far away. Long before the first Russians moved into Siberia, the Mongols of the Great Khans could have taken it over. But they did not want it, being contented occasionally to send expeditions up northward into the forest and tundras in order to swap for furs.

Russia in Europe, the heart of the Soviet country, is a part of the great central plain whose inhabitants have never been willing to stay at home. But by the time the ancestors of the present Russians got around to expansion, the ways were closed to the west by Balts and Germans and Poles and Swedes, to the southwest by the Balkan peoples, to the south by the Black Sea, the Caspian Sea and high mountains, to the east by Mongolian deserts and the impenetrable human masses of China. Only to the north and northeast was the way open, and the Russians took it, until they had explored and taken nominal possession of almost the entire Eurasian coast of the Arctic Ocean, for which, as above stated, at the time nobody else would have given six rubles.

In fact, classifying the Soviets of 1939 as a Two-Ocean Power is a considerable strain on words. Their one real ocean was the selfsame Arctic, most of which is frozen tight for several months a year. Soviet outlets on the Pacific were real enough, except that Vladivostok lies at the end of a long tongue of land stretching right around alien Manchuria, is badly threatened by Japan and closed in winter; while Komsomolsk is situated miles up a frigid stream. Petropavlovsk, near the southern tip of the Kamchatka peninsula, was out in the fogs nearly a thousand miles from anywhere, in an almost totally uninhabited country and completely inaccessible by land. All of which made it difficult for Russia to develop sea power in the Pacific.

Its riparian situation in Europe was hardly better. Murmansk, most westerly of Soviet ports on the Arctic, is kept fluid by the last mild breath of the Gulf Stream, but Archangel, further inland, is icebound each winter. Kronstadt, on the Gulf of Finland, is an opening on an alley. To reach the wide oceans of the world you have to push by Finnish Helsinki and Esthonian Talinn, and then you have only got into the Baltic and are dependent on the goodwill of Germans and Swedes and Danes and Norwegians and Britishers. Nor was it any different in the southwest. The Caspian is a briny lake, the Black Sea a large bay funneling into another inland sea, the Mediterranean, whose exits are also in the hands of alien peoples. In other words, save by world federation or gigantic conquests, Russia simply could not reach the Atlantic. It remained a continental country, with the advantages and discomforts of the same. This is shown by its development: so long as history was the Eastern Hemisphere (Europe, Asia, Africa), Russia was a mighty force. When, during the nineteenth century, the center of civilization shifted to the Atlantic, Russian inability to develop powerful war fleets and sail the seas showed itself a terrible handicap.

It remained for the airplane to give back to the Russians all that unlimited seafaring had taken from them—and more besides. Aviation was not only turning their territories into a key area, but it was giving them their own country, for the first time entirely accessible. Thanks to the airplane, whole towns sprang up along the broad Siberian rivers near the frozen ocean, towns whose inhabitants passed a portion of their twenty-two-hour winter nights playing collective chess by radio, one against the other. Russian ships brought from Arctic port to Arctic port during the brief summer months all those bulky things that the airplanes of 1939 still could not carry.

In fact, by its unique location and area, its land access to most of Europe and every part of Asia, Soviet Russia was the air country of the Eastern Hemisphere par excellence.

To the airman and to him alone, high mountains are just minor obstacles, deserts just landscapes and frozen oceans preferable to open seas. The airlines of the future will span the planet, following the shortest distances. Most of the world's land and inhabitants are in the northern half. The Arctic Area will become a center of air traffic. Practically all Arctic routes touch Soviet territory at one point or other.

In an age of air power the Flying Bear seemed almost bound to come into his own.

JAPAN

From their obscure beginnings, the Nipponese have always been truculent as bantams devoured by barnyard imperialism. Though without essential originality, they felt themselves mimetically puissant and called by *Yamato* to greater things.

It was their abiding strength to be scornful of death. It was their misfortune to find themselves perpetually out of step with the age. Geographically, their beautiful little islands lie off the Asiatic Continent much as Britain does off Europe. But while the European mainland was split up into several countries, the Asiatic mainland opposite Japan was nearly all one great country, China. The Japanese could not "divide and rule": they had to conquer or co-operate. Situation and temperament made them fine, bold sailors; though they never developed sailing ships comparable to frigates or clippers, they could doubtless have produced admirable imitations. The Pacific archipelagoes to the southward perpetually croon an invitation to hardy sea-farers to come and take them. But in the Age of Sea Power, while Hindus and Malays were grabbing at the luscious southern islands, xenophobe Japanese shut themselves up behind the swords of their daimyos, and defied all comers to invade islands nobody particularly wanted. Later, when sea power was definitely in decline, the Japanese came to with a jump and set out as conquerors in their well-imitated steel warships and liners, intent on grabbing a *Lebensraum* of their own and eventually virtually dictating peace to kow-towing Americans in Washington, D. C. Profiting by Chinese decadence, in the course of half a century they laid hands on Korea, Formosa, Manchuria, a number of Pacific islands, parts of China—and showed no signs of halting their southward advance.

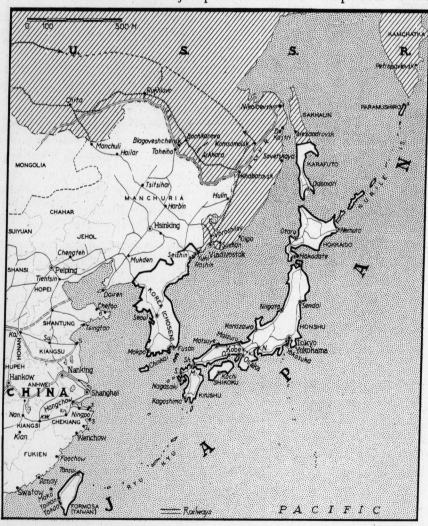

To accomplish their designs, they needed a mighty army—and this their dense population supplied. They also needed vast continental resources of raw materials.

K	Kyoto	S	Sasebo
Ka	Kaifeng	Sh	Shimonoseki
Kn	Kinhwa	Su	Suchow
Kw	Kweiki	1	Shaohing
M	Moji	2	Chinhai
N	Nagoya	3	Shipu
Nan	Nanchang	4	Haimen
O	Okayama	5	Haichow
		6	Weihaiwei

These they obtained in part from Korea and Manchuria on the Asiatic mainland—but only in part. Finally, they needed the innumerable airfields and the air-mindedness that come best of the vast open spaces—and these they just could not create. Do what they would, the Japanese islands remained essentially little islands. The Asiatic mainland was either too cold or too thickly populated to be colonized—at least by Japanese. Therefore, whatever prodigies of self-sacrifice they might accomplish without wincing, only an amazing historical accident could see any large part of their ambitions fulfilled. This accident must permit the *complete* conquest of *all* the territories from which a foe superior in air construction, air tactics and air power could ultimately set about recapturing everything that the Japanese, in one brave rush, had succeeded in laying their hands upon.

This meant that the ultimate safety of Japan depended upon its ability not only to conquer and keep the East Indies, the Malay Peninsula and Australia, but to conquer and keep Indo China, Thailand, Burma and China as well. It was a mammoth ambition, to accomplish which little Japan needed heavy-weight allies and vast pluck.

For Japan simply could not win a defensive war. Once it lost mastery of the air, its island conquests could be retaken from it. Once it lost the islands, it would come to lack oil. Once it was short of oil, it would be driven from the continent of Asia, without access to which it would lack steel. Without air mastery, its powerful fleet could not defend itself against a fleet protected by air power operating from the continent. Once the fleet was gone, air power would allow an invader to land on its coast, coming either from the north or from the south. The moral of that was, Japan must not lose any of the territories from which superior air power could operate.

Even against Soviet Russia alone, the Japanese would be at a grave disadvantage. For the vast Soviet Empire was vulnerable only at its remote center; diminutive Japan was vulnerable almost anywhere it could be hit.

The Japanese were a plucky, though humorless, race. But keeping at arm's length all the enemies Japanese policies were sure to make was bound to be an herculean task.

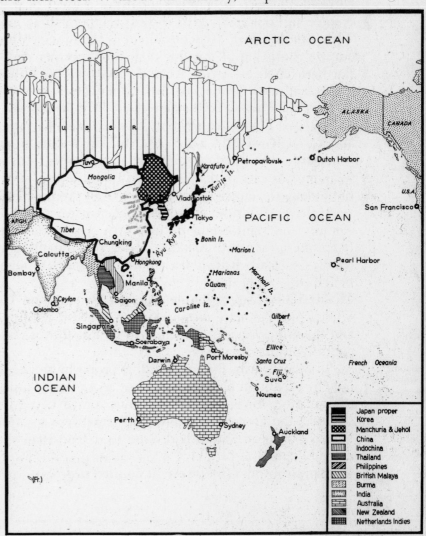

FRANCE

France is the most ideally located country in Europe and the finest piece of that magnificent continent. Of its six sides, five are "natural" frontiers, the English Channel, the Atlantic Ocean, the Pyrenees Mountains, the Mediterranean, the Alps with the River Rhine. Only the sixth side, toward the German Palatinate and Belgium, is largely a haphazard affair and no natural barrier against attack. This was the door through which the Franks and Burgundians poured into Roman Gaul. It is also the route taken subsequently by Germans. In French common talk, the road to Belgium was known as the "route of the invasions."

On the other hand, from France one can invade Southern Germany without much difficulty; or pour into Italy down the Alpine passes that are nearly all in France; or hold the Pyrenees and invade Spanish Catalonia by sea; or so torment Britain by air and submarine attack as to place that country in grave danger of starvation.

France was a definitely balanced country: balanced between industry and agriculture, balanced between continental and overseas interests. Though never supreme on the water, French sailors built up a great overseas empire, with outposts as far distant as India and Canada. Most of this empire was lost to Britain in the eighteenth century, for when the French allowed their sea power to lapse, the amphibian English chipped off piece after piece until not a great deal of it was left. With and under Napoleon, France extended its sway temporarily to most of Europe—and lost it again. Then, undismayed, French soldiers in the nineteenth century built up a new French empire consisting of not less than thirty-six per cent of the surface of Africa. The northern coast of Africa from the Atlantic to Italian Tripolitania was in French hands, and most of the vast Sahara. This territory was a vast reservoir of admirable soldiers, the Moors and the Senegalese of West Africa. This empire was a masterpiece. Continental France with North Africa made a harmonious whole, and after Germany and Soviet Russia, the most powerful single nation on the European continent.

Against any single enemy an alert France thoroughly equipped with modern weapons was easy to defend. And in addition to its seas and mountains, the French built along the entire German frontier an "impregnable" Maginot Line.

If driven from the mainland by Germans, a well-trained French army could find comfort and reinforcements in North Africa and continue a defensive war almost indefinitely, or until Britain, under the impelling need of never permitting any country to flank British sea communications through the Mediterranean by continental expansion, should come to France's assistance and make the south shore of the Mediterranean impregnable. Against Britain, the United States or Japan, on the other hand, the more distant French overseas holdings like Indo China, Madagascar and the minor islands were sure to be lost. But no one of these countries could successfully invade France.

In other words, France could, if properly prepared and on the alert, be defeated only by a coalition between Germany and a Power superior on the sea—a most unlikely combination. Inventive, adventurous, brave beyond the average, truculent, highly civilized, the French for a thousand years were a nation of warriors.

No European nation had more to defend than the French or could more easily defend themselves by taking a few major precautions. Failure to take any one of them was dangerous: to neglect several pointed to defeat; to fail in all was to invite a debacle.

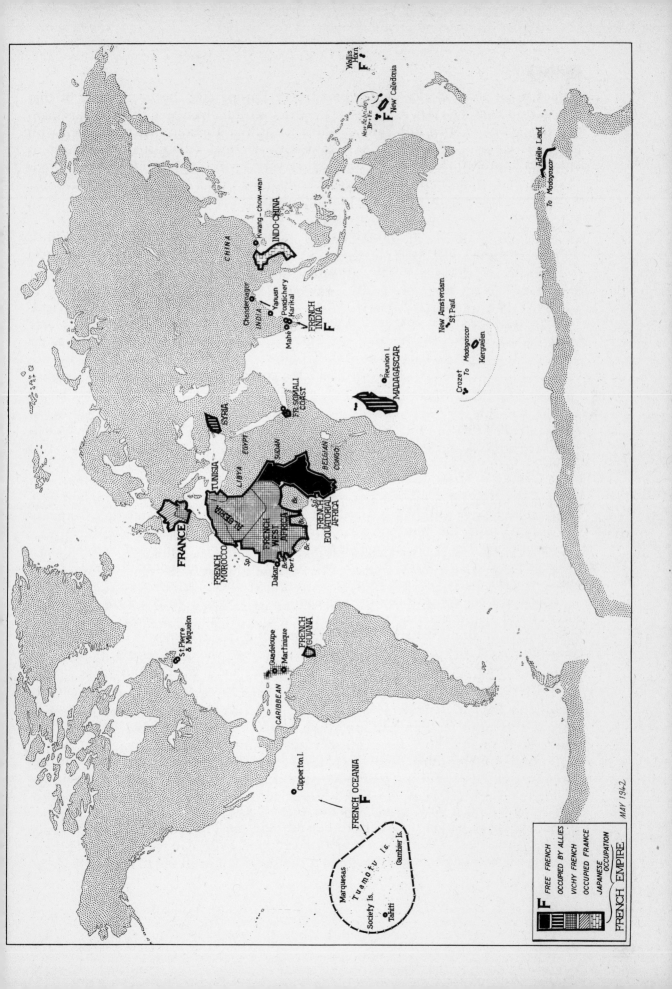

FRENCH EMPIRE   MAY 1942

F FREE FRENCH
OCCUPIED BY ALLIES
VICHY FRENCH
OCCUPIED FRANCE
JAPANESE OCCUPATION

GERMANY

The German Reich, whether First, Second or Third, is emphatically a political reality; it is not a geographical concept. Its only natural frontiers are the Baltic Sea, the North Sea, the Rhine, the Alps, and the Sudeten Mountains. But it failed to fill out its "natural space" by winning over the Danes and the Dutch (who would rather be dead than German), and it spilled over the Rhine into the Palatinate and overran the Alps and the Sudetens, while to the east it was itself "invaded" and alloyed by non-Germanic Prussians, and seriously "infiltrated" by Slavic Wends, Czechs, Poles, etc. Perhaps for this reason a "reich" is something that exists not as so much territory bounded by other territories, but in the German mind. In this respect, otherwise Germanic Swiss and Austrians are definitely not German.

Perhaps, too, this lack of precise frontiers made Germany a place whose inhabitants were always going somewhere else, preferably by attacking their neighbors. If too weak to attack, they emigrated.

The land is neither rich nor poor in natural resources; the inhabitants are competent beyond the average and have made a great deal of it. They take to hard work almost as readily as to fighting.

Germany's two North Sea ports, though well situated, are obviously cramped for space and lie off the main lines. Nothing but mastery of Great Britain could enable Germany to rule the seas (and by sending the Normans into England, God had apparently intended that the English were not to be Germans). The Germans would have preferred to have the British share their empire without a fight. When the British incomprehensibly refused, the Germans twice attacked them, in 1914 and in 1939.

Geographically, Germany's true importance lies in the fact that from here you can get to France, Belgium, Holland, Denmark, Sweden, Poland, Finland, the Baltic countries, Czechoslovakia, Austria, Italy and Switzerland with no trouble at all, and not necessarily to pillage. The land was made to be a rail and air center; in other words, a country of trade and transport and tourists, like Switzerland.

Instead, the Germans have more often thought of their home as a center of power, whose benefits they were destined—by violence when necessary—to spread over ever larger and larger concentric circles. This was a conceit that so fascinated Adolf Hitler's friend, Karl Haushofer, that he seized upon it and made of it first a *problem,* then a *theory,* then a *system* of political domination, called *Geopolitik.* The aim of *Geopolitik* is to demonstrate that the population of Germany can—and therefore should— expand over Europe, Asia, and Africa, the three lobes of a common "world island."

For it can be readily demonstrated that Germans, however peace-loving, can never be safe on their undefendable east without possession of Poland. And having got Poland, they must push onward across the limitless plain into Russia. Having eliminated the Russian danger, Germans will still find themselves threatened by all sorts of ill-mannered Mongolians and Turks from Central Asia. And beyond these live the Chinese, and the limit is the Bering Strait, unless you have the means to get across.

Or, to make it still more simple: Germany, as *Mitteleuropa,* is inevitably encircled. Instead of accepting this with its good and bad consequences the Germans preferred to try vainly to solve the problem: how can the center of a circle swallow the circumference?

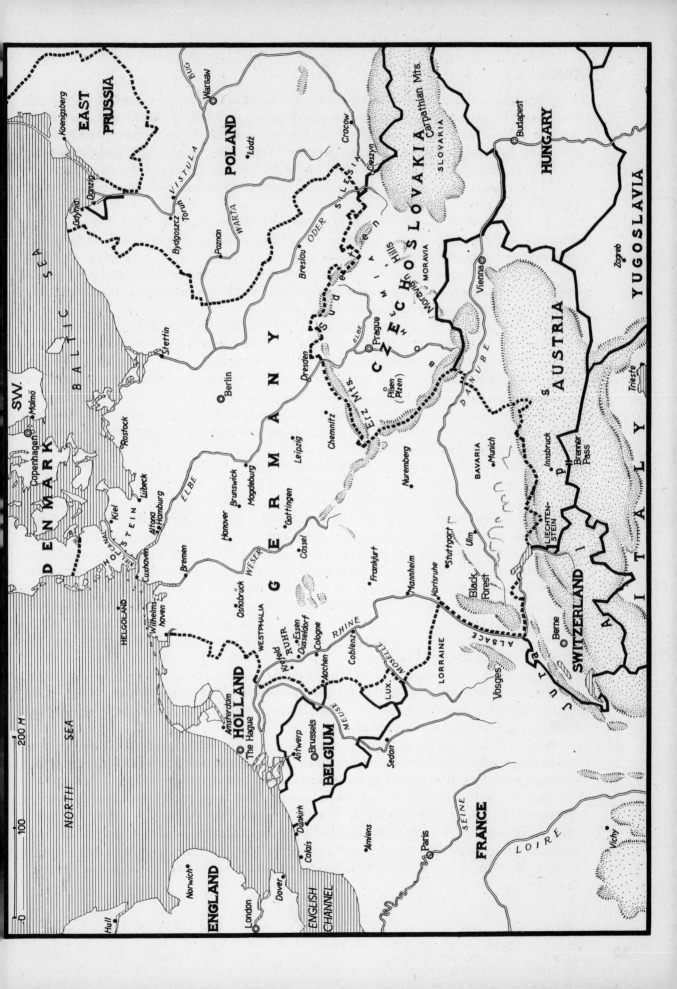

ITALY

Italy has twice been the hub of the Occidental World. In the Classical days, with Western civilization clustered around the glaucous billows of the Mediterranean, it was marvellously located to be the seat of Empire. And again, in the late Middle Ages, its hardy maritime peoples, Pisans, Genoese, Venetians, established great chains of far-flung trading bases. Yet Italy—even under the sturdy ancient Romans, who established universal hegemony and held it until their descendants lost their will to rule—was often invaded.

The discovery of the Atlantic sea routes, the ocean roads to the Far East and to America, turned Italy into a fruit-growing promontory in a backwash—a country full of nostalgic memories of past achievements in every field, magnificent with (more or less ruined) monuments and artistic masterpieces, but with a people rapidly succumbing to the "over-developed sense of self-preservation" that, whatever it proves of intelligence, does not make for high-class fighting men.

Modern Italians divide into two sorts—the masses and the others. The former work hard and well—when they are let alone. But they abhor war, and conquest leaves them cold unless it be bloodless. Their strength lies in their inexhaustible propensity for reproduction. The others—the *signori*—occasionally reach genius in all known human fields, but remain as a class deficient in the will to self-sacrifice.

Sunshine, blue sea, landscapes, beautiful women, natural intelligence, however attractive, do not in a competitive world make a satisfactory substitute for courage, energy and large industrial resources.

The cutting of the Suez Canal and the development of the airplane restored some of Italy's lost geographical advantage. Italy was once more on a main highway. The Italians developed a good merchant marine and might well have become leaders in the air—had they been content to work for quality—like the Swiss. But they could not forget past grandeur and their dreams were not of hard-won prosperity—difficult for so poor a land!—or of a leading place in a United Europe (which they could, perhaps, have achieved) but of a new overseas empire. So the Italians picked out a couple of easy victims and got one. But alas, so long as Italy itself remained within a foreign-dominated Mediterranean, the overseas extra-Mediterranean possessions could not be defended, especially not against a stronger sea power. Italy had, therefore, to dominate the entire Mediterranean and its gates or to confine its empire to nearby territories. And Italy did neither.

Aviation was reducing the Mediterranean from a great sea to a mere inland waterway where ships were badly exposed to land-based air attack. On the other hand, any localities for at least 50 miles inland (shaded on the map) could easily be bombed from the sea by carrier-based planes.

Italy itself was almost as badly placed for defense as for expansion. Warships protected by land-based fighters could make hash of its many coastal towns. Night bombers could easily reach its most inland cities.

To the north, the Alps are far less a barrier than appears on the map. Passes are numerous and relatively accessible. For this reason, the fertile Po Valley has been one of Europe's chosen cockpits, especially since it forms a section of one of the best west-east routes on that continent. Friendship with Germany could ward off this danger. But the threat from North Africa, to which Italy forms a "natural bridge," remained.

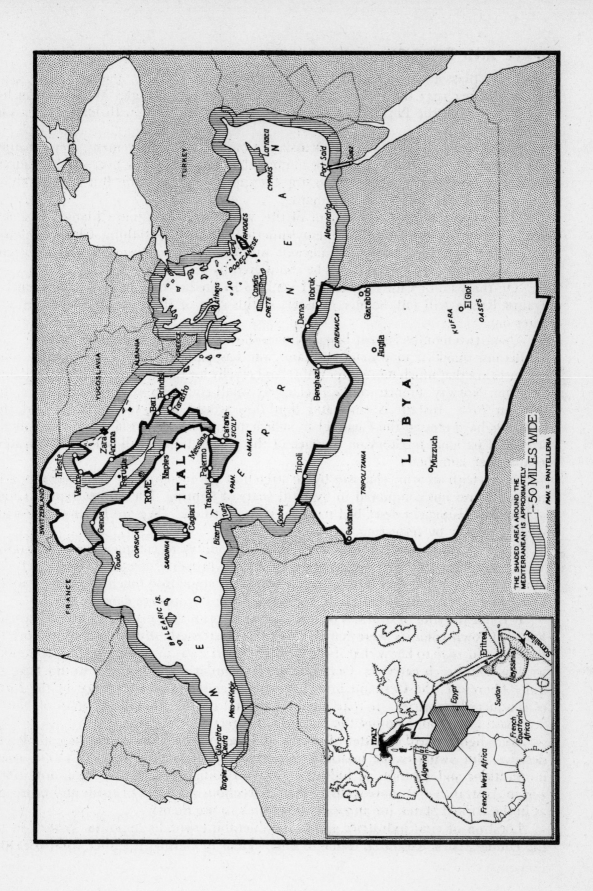

THE SHADED AREA AROUND THE
MEDITERRANEAN IS APPROXIMATELY
↦ 50 MILES WIDE →

PAN. = PANTELLERIA

SPACE AND SECURITY

Sheer area plays a most important part in modern war.

In October 1941 the author was talking with General Douglas MacArthur at his Headquarters in the Philippines. The general paced the floor with long strides and spoke:

"The German offensive against Russia is a magnificent achievement. Never before has an offensive of such magnitude been nourished for such a time over such distances. Generally, an attacking army has to stop for supplies to come up. But not this time. It is a logistic triumph for the Germans.

"The other greatest achievement of this war is Generalissimo Chiang Kai-shek's defense of his country against an enemy superior in nearly everything. China's defense has proven that a people with sufficient numbers, sufficient *morale* and sufficient space to retreat into simply cannot be conquered by any *Blitz*.

"On the base of China's defense I venture to predict that the German offensive against Russia will fail. Sooner or later, at this spot or that, it will bog down and peter out."

About two months later it bogged down short of Moscow and petered out.

Because modern motor-cum-airplane war has partially annihilated space, long distances are that much more important. And chiefly for the defense. Poland, Holland, Belgium, Norway, France were all relatively small countries—and succumbed to the German *Blitz*. Britain is tiny—and doubtless would have succumbed could the Germans have crossed the Channel in sufficient force. But Russia, the vastest single stretch of national territory on the face of the globe, did not fall before the greatest assault ever launched.

China, with an army that can by no stretch of the imagination be called properly equipped, was not conquered in five full years of fighting. For as the Deputy Chief of Staff Pei Hsung-chi described national strategy to me: "We are buying time with space"—namely by retreating.

The United States is an extremely difficult country to conquer. So is Australia. So is India with less area, but still plenty. Brazil, properly defended, could defy an immense army of invaders. On the other hand it is enough to touch Japan or Italy to bring about collapse—as the loss of Malaya and the Philippines demonstrated.

It is not the sum of overseas or scattered territories that matters. The widespread British Crown colonies were hardly a source of strength. But it was a comfort to Britishers in 1940 to know that if the mother country was overrun, the vast Commonwealths could each carry on. Germany, under similar circumstances, would have to quit. Therefore, the Germans first cushioned themselves with distance in the form of conquered countries. In 1942, save by air and on the single brief strip of North Sea coast, none could wound the Fatherland directly.

Were fighting still a matter of swords and spears, area alone might be completely decisive. But owing to the insatiable requirements of modern fighting forces, communications and location of industries are very important. Scant communications —as in Australia—give more security than marvellous networks of roads and railroads as in the United States, for an assailant is quick to use them.

Location of vital industries grants invulnerability—or its opposite. Where, as in the United States, Australia, India, to some extent in Germany, China, industries are

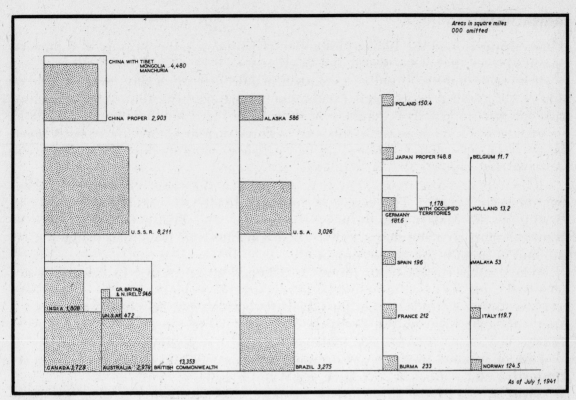

Areas in square miles
000 omitted

CHINA WITH TIBET MONGOLIA MANCHURIA 4,480

CHINA PROPER 2,903

ALASKA 586

POLAND 150.4

JAPAN PROPER 148.8

BELGIUM 11.7

U.S.S.R. 8,211

U.S.A. 3,026

GERMANY 181.6

1,178 WITH OCCUPIED TERRITORIES

HOLLAND 13.2

SPAIN 196

MALAYA 53

INDIA 1,808

GR. BRITAIN & N. IRELD 94.6

U.N.S.AE 472

FRANCE 212

ITALY 119.7

CANADA 3,728

AUSTRALIA 2,974

13,353 BRITISH COMMONWEALTH

BRAZIL 3,275

BURMA 233

NORWAY 124.5

As of July 1, 1941

LAND AREA

somewhat peripheral, national defense is weaker by that much. Where they are central —as in part in Russia—the defense factor rises.

Climate and topography are also important though less than before. Alaskan cold and mountains still combine to give some protection to that large territory. In the Sahara, heat and sand do the same, though the flat *hammada* or stony desert allows specially equipped motor vehicles to pass.

The distance-devouring quality of modern war engines has perhaps sounded the requiem for little countries as fully independent units.

MANPOWER

Three elements, said the Italian philosopher Umano, give the measure of a modern nation's power: numbers, wealth and intelligence.

It is not a complete formula—it excludes morale—but it is a good working rule of thumb. Other things being equal, numbers of population mean abundance of fighting men and war workers. It is thanks to its multitudes that China has more or less held its own against a more powerful adversary. Three or four Chinese have been killed for every Japanese. But China had enough people to stand the loss. India can do the same—at least theoretically. So can Soviet Russia—and does.

Generally speaking, in modern times, one must consider only self-governing States, not subjected peoples. The masses of India, if disaffected, could be a liability to Britain—as the Malays and Burmese often were. The British Commonwealth of Nations suffers an acute shortage of United Kingdom and Dominion manpower its millions of subordinate people cannot fill.

Where subject populations cannot be counted on or trusted to fight, they are nonetheless an asset in the industrial production. Frenchmen, Czechs, Poles, Norwegians, cannot be made to fight for Germany: but they can be starved into working after a fashion. Their output swells the war potential of the erstwhile master. East Indians may or may not be good soldiers, but their war production is very real.

Lack of area and relatively small numbers doomed Poland to defeat even had its equipment and military service been equal to Germany's.

Soviet Russia's large and relatively homogeneous population is, after its space, its greatest asset. Holes in the ranks, however gaping, can be filled. Though thousands of aviators and parachutists are lost, more are always just behind them.

The fear of Japan deep in the heart of every Australian is based on the Commonwealth's self-centered neglect of the population problem. Seven million occupy a territory that could support fifty. Fifty million Australians could defy Japan. In Japan seventy-three millions live crowded together on a territory fit for at most forty or fifty millions.

Predatory peoples have always recognized the value of numbers. Hitler aimed at a homogeneous group of two hundred and fifty million Germans in Europe. The over-crowded Italians rewarded childbearing. The Japanese, though they are reluctant to emigrate, continually whine about their lack of space. Aggressor peoples formulate their own philosophy: Our territory is too small for our present population, but let us have still more babies, and we can conquer new territories to expand into!

"Mere" numbers has, in many places, become an expression almost of contempt. This shows fearful lack of discernment. Far wiser the ancient dictum: In numbers there is strength.

WORLD POPULATION

Legend:
- ■ Self governing
- ▥ Controlled
- ▦ Under occupation

Figures are in millions

MIDDLE EAST

PALESTINE 1.4 TR.J. 0.3
IRAQ 3.1
AFGHANISTAN 7
SYRIA 3.6
SAUDI ARABIA 7
IRAN 15
TURKEY 17

PORTUGAL
103
6.8

SPAIN
1
25.6

ITALY
0.8
43

FRENCH EMPIRE

OTHER (NEGLIGIBLE)
SYRIA LEBANON 3.6
MADAGASCAR 3.9
FR. EQ. AFRICA 3.5
FR. W. AFRICA 14.8
NORTH AFRICA 15.6
INDOCHINA 23
FRANCE 42

EUROPE

4 1 3 . 8 TOTAL EUROPE & TURKEY*

UNITED KINGDOM 47.6
TURKEY 17
EIRE 2.9
SWEDEN 6.3
SWITZERLAND 4.2
PORTUGAL 7.4
SPAIN 25.6
FINLAND 4

YUGOSLAVIA 15.5
HUNGARY 10
BULGARIA 6.2
GREECE 7.1
RUMANIA 20
BALTIC COUNTRIES 5.5
DENMARK & NORWAY 6.6
BELGIUM 8.3
FRANCE 42
HOLLAND 8.2

POLAND 35
CZECHOSLOVAKIA 15.7 1 7 0 . 4
AUSTRIA 7

UNDER ENEMY OCCUPATION
ITALY 43
GERMANY REICH 69.4 (1939)

U.S.S.R.

CHINA

4 5 7 8
NORTHEASTERN PROVS.
OUTLYING POSSES'NS
UNDER JAP CONTROL IN CHINA PROPER (ESTIMATE)

4 5 7
30
40

U.S.A.

1 4 9
OUTLYING POSSESSIONS 18.7

JAPANESE EMPIRE

2 2 4 . 1
BURMA 15.9
NETH. INDIES 68.4
THAILAND 14.9
BRITISH MALAYA 5.2
INDOCHINA 23.5
PHILIPPINES 16.2
MANCHURIA, JEHOL & ESTIMATED CONTROLLED POPULATION IN CHINA 80

CENT. & S. AMERICA

1 3 3 . 1
OTHERS C. AM. CARIB.
MEXICO 20
1 0 4 . 3
OUTLYING POSSESSIONS 31.5
VENEZUELA 3.5
COLOMBIA 8.8
ARGENTINA 12.9
BRAZIL 44
72.7

MEXICO

MAY 42

BRIT. COMMONWEALTH

5 2 1 . 9
REST OF EMPIRE¹ 96.6
DOMINIONS 24.9
UNITED KINGDOM 47.6

INDIA 352.8

5

---

¹For British Malaya, Burma, Hongkong under enemy occupation see last column.

*Without European Russia.

¹Without European Russia.

WEALTH

Wealth is by no means the last word in war, but Umano rightfully put it among the decisive commensurable elements. A man with a moneybag may have to submit to a man with a club: but under most circumstances the man of money finds little difficulty in hiring two men with clubs to protect him. Global War does not permit much hiring—there are so few sources of man power normally not involved. But there can be little doubt but that Powers with the capacity to supply raw materials, engines of war, munitions, food and manufactured articles, or able without strain to buy up commercial surpluses or guarantee against later financial losses, find it easier to acquire allies. In war, money talks twice as loud.

RAW MATERIALS

The war potentials of a nation actually fighting is largely a question of its industry. But during a struggle the industrial exponent can neither be closely ascertained nor properly published. Peoples at war push the manufacture of airplanes, motor vehicles, ships, a thousand sorts of military material far beyond anything seen or even imagined in time of peace, and the total figure is constantly changing.

One good clue to the relative industrial strength of nations would seem to be the one here chosen, namely, the production of raw materials. A glance at the accompanying graph will show that in 1942 the United Nations topped the Axis and Axis-controlled countries in supplies of most essential things: two-thirds of the coal of the world; sixty per cent of the total pig iron production; nearly two-thirds of the steel; most of the manganese (and with India, four-fifths of it); more chrome, more tungsten, more antimony and infinitely more mineral oil. The Axis—thanks to conquered supplies—led in available aluminum, in tin and in rubber. (This last detail seems an overwhelming demonstration of why automobile tires had to be rationed in the United Nations.)

Obviously, this is not all the picture. Raw materials at home are infinitely more desirable than those that must be transported vast distances, especially by water at a time when submarines are prowling the Seven Seas looking for freighters to sink. In this respect the Axis had an advantage. The materials it utilized were either actually in its possession or contiguous (Sweden, Switzerland, Spain). The Axis had virtually no problem of ocean shipping.

Obviously, it wished that it did—namely, that it had sea connection between its European and its Asiatic centers, between Hamburg, say, and Tokyo. For while Tokyo could squander conquered rubber, German trucks were immobilized for lack of tires.

Admittedly, in the transmutation of raw materials into war materials, numerous imponderables, vital energy, aptitude, habit, morale, are highly important. American workmen produce more in a given time with the same equipment than Russian workmen. So do Germans.

Yet where peoples are more or less equal in capacity, availability of vital raw materials is a measure of effective wealth.

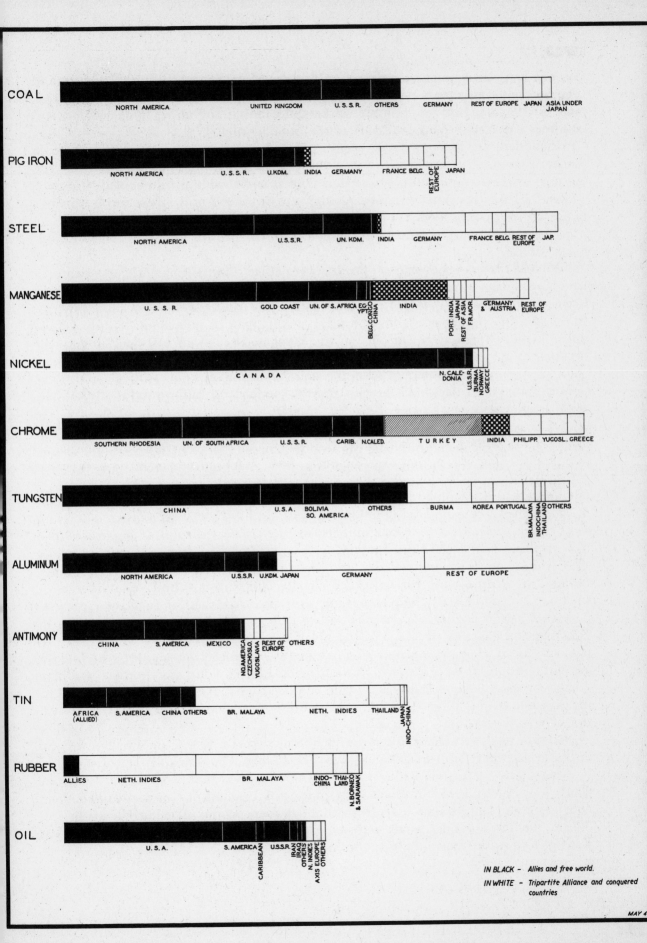

COAL — NORTH AMERICA · UNITED KINGDOM · U.S.S.R. · OTHERS · GERMANY · REST OF EUROPE · JAPAN · ASIA UNDER JAPAN

PIG IRON — NORTH AMERICA · U.S.S.R. · U.KDM. · INDIA · GERMANY · FRANCE BELG. · REST OF EUROPE · JAPAN

STEEL — NORTH AMERICA · U.S.S.R. · UN. KDM. · INDIA · GERMANY · FRANCE BELG. · REST OF EUROPE · JAP.

MANGANESE — U.S.S.R. · GOLD COAST · UN. OF S. AFRICA · EGYPT · BELG. CONGO · CHINA · INDIA · PORT. INDIA · JAPAN · REST OF ASIA · FR. MOR. · GERMANY & AUSTRIA · REST OF EUROPE

NICKEL — CANADA · N. CALEDONIA · U.S.S.R. · BURMA · NORWAY · GREECE

CHROME — SOUTHERN RHODESIA · UN. OF SOUTH AFRICA · U.S.S.R. · CARIB. · N. CALED. · TURKEY · INDIA · PHILIPP. · YUGOSL. · GREECE

TUNGSTEN — CHINA · U.S.A. · BOLIVIA SO. AMERICA · OTHERS · BURMA · KOREA · PORTUGAL · BR. MALAYA · INDOCHINA · THAILAND · OTHERS

ALUMINUM — NORTH AMERICA · U.S.S.R. · U.KDM. · JAPAN · GERMANY · REST OF EUROPE

ANTIMONY — CHINA · S. AMERICA · MEXICO · NO. AMERICA · CZECHOSLO. · YUGOSLAVIA · REST OF EUROPE · OTHERS

TIN — AFRICA (ALLIED) · S. AMERICA · CHINA · OTHERS · BR. MALAYA · NETH. INDIES · THAILAND · JAPAN · INDO-CHINA

RUBBER — ALLIES · NETH. INDIES · BR. MALAYA · INDO-CHINA · THAILAND · N. BORNEO & SARAWAK

OIL — U.S.A. · S. AMERICA · CARIBBEAN · U.S.S.R. · IRAN · IRAQ · OTHERS · N. INDIES · AXIS EUROPE · OTHERS

IN BLACK – Allies and free world.

IN WHITE – Tripartite Alliance and conquered countries

MAY 42

FOOD

Yet, to win a war it is not enough to be able to put into the air and into the ships and into the field vast numbers of keen, courageous, aggressive, well-equipped fighting men. Soldiers must be fed. So must workers in factories and mines. Even women and children and the "dispensable" part of the population.

"Food will win the war and the peace," American Secretary of Agriculture Claude Wickard insisted. It won't. But it will help mightily. Nothing demoralized the Germans quite so quickly in World War One as wretched and insufficient eating.

Despite the American trend away from cereals toward milk, fruit and fresh vegetables, in test periods food still means mostly grains and potatoes. And a glance at the production figure of the principal protagonists of the present war shows several interesting things.

Look at the map showing the production of rice. Both China and Japan, though heavy producers of rice, did not, before the war, grow enough to satisfy their own needs. Both were heavy importers. So long as Indo China was not occupied, China could and did import rice from there. But with Japan in possession of Indo China, not only the Chinese were cut off, but the Japanese needs were satisfied. Subsequent occupation of Thailand and part of what is here shown as India—namely, Burma—gave the Japanese far more rice than they could consume in so far as they could transport it. India never had much surplus and the Netherland Indies produced too little. Rice became scarce in Europe.

Or take wheat. Continental Europe was the greatest producer of wheat on earth, even without Russia. And Continental Europe was, by 1942, entirely Axis dominated. Nonetheless food was lacking over the entire area. For Continental Europe *imported* wheat above its production.

The great wheat exporting countries either made part of the United Nations or their wheat was available to the United Nations, like that of Argentina. Therefore the United Nations were as much embarrassed by a wheat surplus as Japan was by a rice surplus. Canada, the United States, Argentina, Australia, Soviet Russia, normally were wheat exporting countries. By 1942 they suffered acutely from lack of customers, though the growing need for industrial alcohol offered a possibility of relief.

Look now at the little chart on page 32. It is estimated that for 1938-1939, each inhabitant of what became temporarily Axis Europe had at his disposal 932 pounds of potatoes, seven pounds of rice, 157 pounds of rye and 267 pounds of wheat. But this is theory. In practice peasant hoarding considerably reduced the amount available for general consumption. Bad transportation made life hard for city-dwellers. German seizure of food stocks everywhere made it catastrophic for all European non-Axis peoples. On the other hand, the conquerors were clearly not going to starve with such stocks of food available.

Russian food and potato supplies were about adequate before the war, but the loss of the heavy wheat growing Ukraine was a bad blow. There was danger of shortage.

The United Kingdom's bitter need of food imports is also apparent from this chart. Less than a pound of potatoes, a quarter of a pound of wheat, available meat and vegetable supplements are not enough to keep people alive, still less efficient. The United States and Canada were able to supply the deficiency. Their problem was not to produce but to deliver the food.

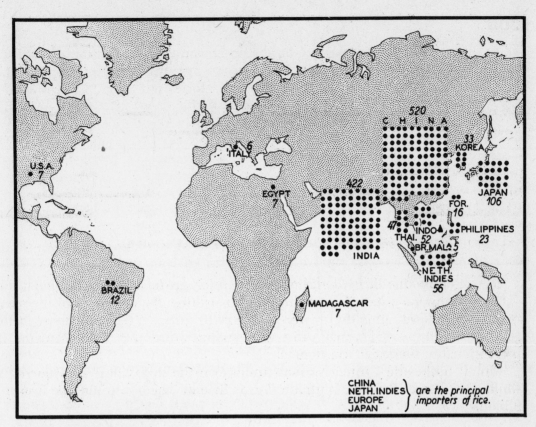

RICE PRODUCTION—1935

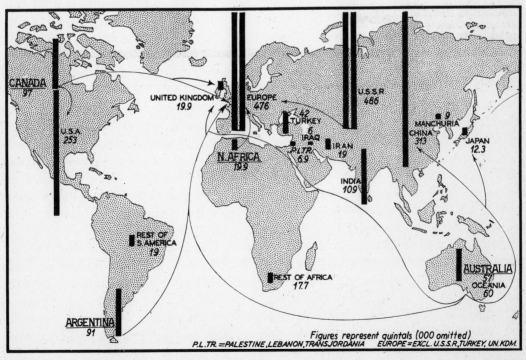

WHEAT PRODUCTION—1937-1941. (Chief exporting countries are underlined.)

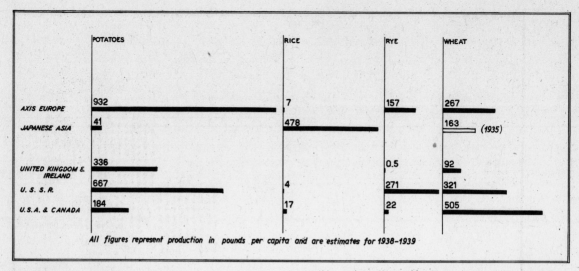

	POTATOES	RICE	RYE	WHEAT
AXIS EUROPE	932	7	157	267
JAPANESE ASIA	41	478		163 (1935)
UNITED KINGDOM & IRELAND	336		0.5	92
U.S.S.R.	667	4	271	321
U.S.A. & CANADA	184	17	22	505

All figures represent production in pounds per capita and are estimates for 1938-1939

Here, as this other little chart shows, was Hitler's great chance. Continental Europe —Hitler's temporary domain—required less than three dollars' worth of merchandise imported per head annually to survive, if not to prosper. Great Britain, including Eire, absolutely needed nearly thirty-one dollars' worth per head. Wartime needs unquestionably increased the figures.

Moral: unless the United Nations could keep the ships afloat and moving, they would lose Great Britain. Without Great Britain victory would be worse than dubious.

Continental Europe (Including whole of Europe & Turkey, USSR excl.) $2.75

United Kingdom & Eire (before Sept. 1.1939) $30.91

GOLD RESERVES

Another source of wealth, gold reserves available for cash payments, was not really important in this war, and for two reasons. First, the United States had nearly all of it. When one player gets all the chips they cease to count or the game is over. And in war time, under the threat of creeping scarcity, peoples have a way of preferring real consumable things—food, for instance—to cold yellow metal.

Interesting in this chart is its demonstration how the United States, possessing in 1938 most of the world's gold reserves, increased them until 1941 when Lend-Lease operations obviated most transfers of gold.

Second among possessors of gold was France with two billion dollars, a large share of which was in the care of Vichy Admiral Robert, on the Island of Martinique.

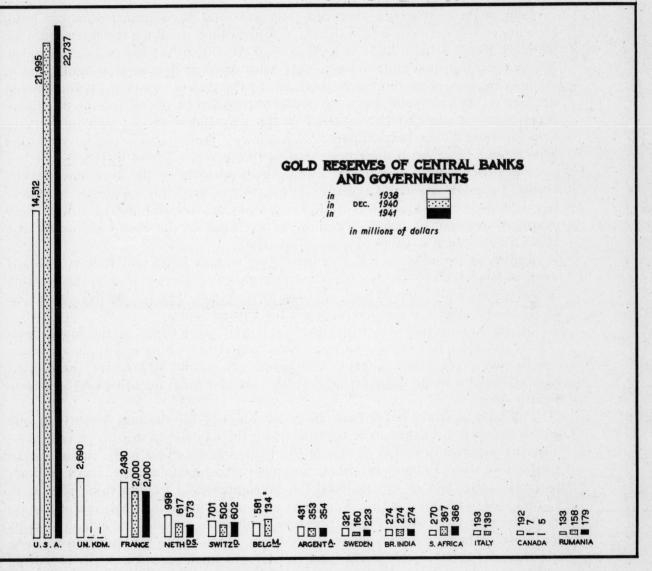

GOLD RESERVES OF CENTRAL BANKS AND GOVERNMENTS

in — 1938
in — DEC. 1940
in — 1941

in millions of dollars

U.S.A.: 14,512 / 21,995 / 22,737
UN. KDM.: 2,690
FRANCE: 2,430 / 2,000 / 2,000
NETH.DS.: 998 / 617 / 573
SWITZ.D.: 701 / 502 / 602
BELG.M.: 581 / 134*
ARGENT.A.: 431 / 353 / 354
SWEDEN: 321 / 160 / 223
BR.INDIA: 274 / 274 / 274
S. AFRICA: 270 / 367 / 366
ITALY: 193 / 139
CANADA: 192 / 7 / 5
RUMANIA: 133 / 158 / 179

Note: Figures on the gold holding of the U.S.S.R. are not available.

INCOME

International wealth is essentially a matter of a section of the earth well exploited, but its simplest expression is living standard, or real income. The chart on the opposite page is based on the average real income (1925-1934) of the peoples of the world in a common international unit—U. S. dollars equalized for buying power—which thus shows not the absolute but the relative wealth*.

On this chart the United States leads the world with 1381 units of real income per head. Here lies the fundamental basis of American strength in modern mechanized war. Canada is a close second with another Dominion, New Zealand, right behind. Irresistible nations, what? But look at the table at the right. All three together—shown in black on the map—account for but *140 million people*. Their manpower, though not small, is definitely limited.

Look at the next section—between 1000 and 1200 international units per head. Here are even fewer people—less than sixty-four million in all. Of the three countries included, Great Britain, little Switzerland and Argentina, the last two were neutral. Between 900 and 1000 units you have only Australia's less than seven millions, and in the next category (800-900) the Netherlands by themselves, representing the greatest affluence on the continent of Europe thanks to commercial genius and the intelligent exploitation of vast and rich colonies in the East Indies (whose own inhabitants, however, come in the lowest category here shown). From 700-800 you have another little country, Eire—with some strategical significance as a key to Britain.

The richer part of continental Europe lives normally at the next lower level—France, Denmark, Sweden, Germany (thus destroying any illusions about "have-not" Germany and "rich" France). Together they make nearly two hundred million well-educated, well-trained people. Belgium, at the head of the group following, also benefits by overseas colonies of giant proportions.

And so on through the list. It is interesting to find Japan and Italy at virtually the same level. Both peoples are really short of territory yet seek to remedy the situation by forcing multiplication at home and conquest abroad. The people live about one-fourth as abundantly as the inhabitants of the United States.

British India comes at a still lower level. And giant China at the lowest level (120 units). Here is, however, an interesting conjecture: China and India are about equally rich in potential resources, intelligence, and people. If, however, the Indians have achieved a living standard high above that of China, may this not be due to British rule?

The most startling fact I have, however, reserved for the last. More than one half of the earth's inhabitants are grouped with the Chinese in this lowest category—standard one-seventh or less of that of the United States. This is the sub-industrial level (or nearly). In modern times, unindustrialized peoples have small military potential unless lack of war material can be compensated by something else, as in China's case. The point is that, as matters now stand, more than half the people on earth live at a level which almost pre-destines them to conquest or exploitation by the more energetic or more fortunate peoples. Their choice is—according to these statistics—industrial development (and conceivably birth-control as well) or lasting weakness.

*Most of these figures are taken from *The Conditions of Economic Progress* by Colin Clark, The Macmillan Company, New York, 1940. Figures for Argentina, India and China are estimated.

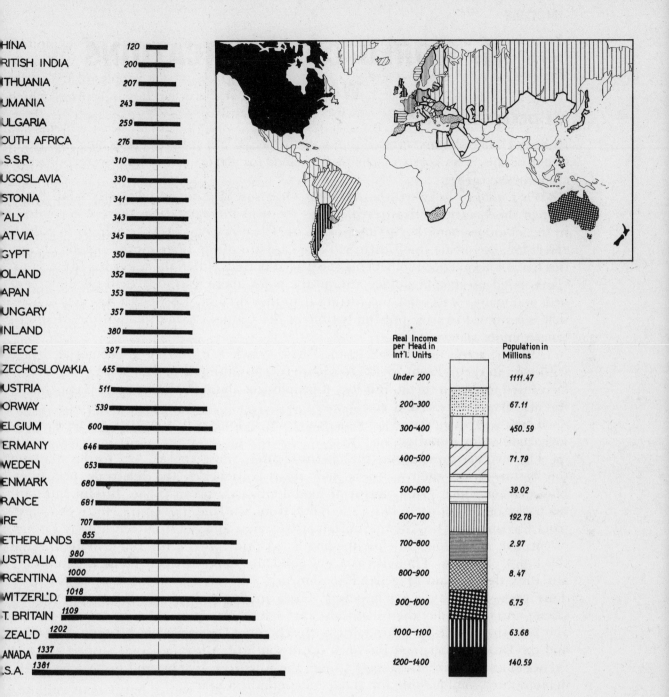

CHINA 120
BRITISH INDIA 200
LITHUANIA 207
RUMANIA 243
BULGARIA 259
SOUTH AFRICA 276
U.S.S.R. 310
YUGOSLAVIA 330
ESTONIA 341
ITALY 343
LATVIA 345
EGYPT 350
POLAND 352
JAPAN 353
HUNGARY 357
FINLAND 380
GREECE 397
CZECHOSLOVAKIA 455
AUSTRIA 511
NORWAY 539
BELGIUM 600
GERMANY 646
SWEDEN 653
DENMARK 680
FRANCE 681
EIRE 707
NETHERLANDS 855
AUSTRALIA 980
ARGENTINA 1000
SWITZERL'D. 1018
GT. BRITAIN 1109
N. ZEAL'D 1202
CANADA 1337
U.S.A. 1381

Real Income per Head in Int'l. Units	Population in Millions
Under 200	1111.47
200-300	67.11
300-400	450.59
400-500	71.79
500-600	39.02
600-700	192.78
700-800	2.97
800-900	8.47
900-1000	6.75
1000-1100	63.68
1200-1400	140.59

II. WORLD COMMUNICATIONS
WATERWAYS

ALL-OCEAN SEA LANES

Nobody knows who first crossed the Atlantic Ocean, but it happened a long time ago. Other oceans, with coasts or chains of islands for navigators to hug, were probably crossed even earlier.

What used to be called the Antarctic Ocean turned out to be mostly land. Even though the Continent thus revealed was too cold for habitation, there was comfort in the announcement. For to most of us, the Creator seems overly generous to sailors and fishes, bestowing upon them too large a share of the surface of the globe. True, this has not always been so. During the glacial periods, when the water has been, so to speak, piled up in cold storage around the poles, there was less left to fill the ocean beds and many coasts stuck out further than they do now. I believe it was melting ice that is supposed to have put the bottom of the China Sea and some of the Mediterranean under water.

Anyway, across all this salt vastness have crawled, from time immemorial, boats with men in them. From kayaks to square-rigged sailing-men, they were not particularly fitted for ocean travel. But lots of peoples got about in them just the same, heedless of scurvy, tempests and *mal-de-mer*.

There is no evidence of a people going soft so long as its sons took to the sea—for love, and not for subsidies.

The striking thing about the oceans—as they must appear, say, to the Man in the Moon—is less their vastness than their bottlenecks, the relatively few spots possession of which gives control of most long-range ocean traffic. Britain built its sea power on its ability to block the Baltic from Scotland, the entire North Sea coast from England, and the Mediterranean at Gibraltar and Suez. Fifteen hundred miles of effective sea patrols can close the South Atlantic between the Bulge of Brazil and the Bulge of Africa. Though passage around the Cape of Good Hope is exceptionally easy, that around Magellan-Cape Horn is a terror, and avoided when possible. This is why Panama is a key to power. There are but three channels from the Indian Ocean into the Pacific: the usual route through the Strait of Malacca, past Singapore and into the China Sea; through the treacherous Torres Straits between Australia and the Dutch Indies; and the open ocean south of Australia. Some suspect the existence of a sure northern passage around the Americas; that around Eurasia has been demonstrated semi-feasible for about four months a year.

The fine open-water channel extending right around the globe just north of the Antarctic Continent is next to useless, especially since the opening of the Panama and Suez Canals. For the most part it leads nowhere people care to go or send goods.

Many sea nations have become powerful beyond their apparent strength: Phoenicians, Carthaginians, ancient Greeks, Arabs, Portuguese, Northmen, Spaniards, Genoese, Venetians, Dutch, Japanese, and Englishmen. Without large populations or ample territories, the sea-goers simply staked out systems of heavily fortified bases with

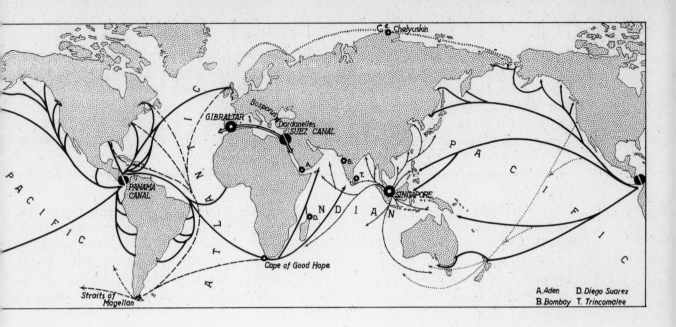

harbors and supply centers from which to operate, without much worry about the hinterlands.

Bases offer shelter, supplies, fuel, repair docks and shops, rest; their possession forces enemy ships to keep away or stay at home.

The nineteenth century saw the height of sea power. Sailing ships reached their supreme technical and esthetic beauty and sailor peoples tattooed an anchor on the breast of the age. Seafaring made for free trade and free trade for prosperity and a single financial system in this case centered in London, capital of the greatest maritime empire.

This so impressed the American admiral, Alfred Thayer Mahan, that he echoed Sir Walter Raleigh to the effect that "world power rested on sea power and commerce." Or as John Adams had flamboyantly proclaimed, "The trident of Neptune is the scepter of the world." (How Alexander and Ghenghis Khan would have laughed!) The theory of Raleigh-Adams-Mahan has been true at times—but only at times.

Consider. In the blessed days before radio, a fleet of sailing ships could put to sea and disappear for many months, turning up as a superior concentration of power at the most unexpected places.

Steamships at sea, plus railroads and, later, motor-driven vehicles on hard roads brought about the decline of sea power. For the steamships could not solve the fuel problem; they could not stay out and cruise about for months. Moreover, even the fastest transports remained slow, compared to locomotives and motor trucks. Finally, bombers, operating protected or unprotected from land bases, could sink ships, while ships could be protected only by fighter planes operating from carriers which needed bases and fueling just like the other ships, and were always inferior to land-based fighter planes. Thus an immense superiority in both offense and defense was bestowed upon a land Power operating on inner lines from a relatively vast, and therefore less vulnerable, territory—as German *Geopolitik* had foreseen.

Some experts looked forward to the virtual disappearance of ships except as pleasure craft, with giant air freighters carrying the world's goods. To others this was a zealot's dream—airplanes in their estimation could supplement but could never replace surface vessels.

All this meant that the maritime bottlenecks became extremely difficult for a purely sea Power to hold, unless navies—notably aircraft carriers and supply ships (and sailors)—could be multiplied by ten or twenty.

Dogmatizing in a changing world is fatuous, but the following opinion can be risked:

Until battleships and ocean freighters become much less vulnerable to under- and over-water attack or can carry their own sufficient air protection; or until land-based fighter planes develop a range comparable to the present range of bombing planes so that they can afford constant protection to ships; or until isolated sea and air bases can be fortified and supplied to withstand months of unlimited land and air attack—what Major de Seversky has called "the twilight of sea power" seems likely to continue—as Admiral Mahan did not foresee.

One may well doubt if there will ever be another dawn and if, as this war progresses, ships of all types will not more and more be superseded by aircraft, for everything from fighting to transporting tanks.

THE LAP OF THE AMERICAS

When, in 1492, Christopher Columbus sailed smack into the island of San Salvador, he did not know that he was thrusting Spain's blood and gold banner into the lap of the Americas.

For a long time thereafter, despite French sea rovers and British buccaneers, Spaniards bossed the Spanish Main—and very rich it made them. For from this central sea they expanded in all directions—into Florida and Mexico, Central America and all of South America save Brazil.

France managed to grab a few of the West Indian prizes and still holds Guadeloupe, Martinique, French Guiana and Mariegalante.

Beginning in the seventeenth century, Britain became supreme here, and eventually welcomed the emancipation of European colonies in the Americas, and inspired the young Government of the United States to proclaim the Monroe Doctrine. This was an Anglo-Saxon partnership aimed at other European countries, and effective primarily in virtue of the good strong British fleet kept permanently in these waters.

At the beginning, the Doctrine did not mean the Americas for the Americans, and Britain kept tight hold of what it possessed and was reluctant to see the United States expand or dig a short-cut canal through the American Isthmus. British holdings included British Honduras and British Guiana on the mainland, and numerous islands: the Windward Group, the Leewards, the Bahamas, and beautiful, impoverished Jamaica.

Yet the attempt to block American ambitions was bound to fail, and for several reasons. First, the cutting of a canal was in the interests of mankind and practically bound to be done sooner or later: opposition to it was thoroughly anti-social. More-

▪ Existing U.S. Bases (outside U.S.)	▬ Mountains above 10000 ft.	∘ Airports or landing fields	— ⋅ — International Boundaries
▭ Defense Base Sites leased by U.S. from Great Britain	▦ Mountains above 2000 ft.	↵ Seaplane anchorages	c. Colombia CR. Costa Rica

over, to the British the Caribbean was just another sea: to the Americans it was home waters and requisite to their safety. Finally, the Anglo-Saxon partnership was vital to both parties.

As the pressure on Britain grew in Europe, willingness to admit American naval supremacy in American waters grew with it. When Admiral Mahan finally formulated his Four Principles of Action for an American Foreign Policy, the first was, naturally, supremacy in the Caribbean, and the fourth, collaboration with Great Britain—which was just what had been going on. In 1901 the British Fleet finally steamed for home and British bases were thenceforth neglected. Years later, in 1914, the Pacific and Atlantic oceans were joined by American efforts. And at this moment, and not before, the United States became a Great Power. When, in the summer of 1940, the British leased to the Americans sites for naval and air bases (among others) at Mayaguana in the Bahamas, at Kingston, Jamaica, at Antigua, Santa

Lucia, Trinidad and at two points in British Guiana, the world took it as a matter of course. Not even the South Americans were alarmed. Though he who holds the Caribbean is master of the hemisphere, by the Good Neighbor Policy the Colossus of the North was proving itself a friendly cousin of the Latin Americans.

The Caribbean, with its inner pantry, the Gulf of Mexico, is a superb piece of water. From the Florida Keys to the mouths of the Orinoco, nearly 2000 miles, the West Indies stretch a sinuous barrier against the Atlantic surge. Two of the major islands, Cuba and Haiti-Santo Domingo, are as large as some American States; Jamaica, Puerto Rico, Trinidad, Bahaman Andros and Abaca are as large as big counties. The rest are diminutive but myriad. Not far to the east, in the Atlantic, is that strange floating vegetable garden, the Sargasso Sea. Behind the islands, to the north and west and south, is relative calm, disturbed only by occasional tornadoes. Into this island sea there are relatively few entrances. The most northerly, the Florida Strait, serves as passage to the outflowing Gulf Stream, and is screened by six hundred miles of coral-reefed Bahamas. Windward Passage, between Cuba and Haiti is dominated by Jamaica. Then comes Mona Passage, sixty miles wide, and deep. From Puerto Rico right down to British-owned Grenada, there are island channels, narrow and easily controlled. Only north of Trinidad the passage is both wide and easy. Few bodies of water in the world should be easier to defend than this against naval- and ship-based air attack.

The United States enjoyed (1942) a perfect chain of naval and air bases, controlling all the important channels, with a big central air base at Jamaica, in the key island of the area. From these bases American sea and air fleets could make the task of an intended invader of the Caribbean extremely hazardous.

On the other hand, multiplicity of islands and harbors, plus good weather and generally clear skies, make this "American Mediterranean" the happy hunting ground of raiding submarines, particularly if they can manage to secure local complicity in the obtaining of fuel and supplies. For the United States, keeping the Caribbean sea lanes open is a *must*.

THE PANAMA CANAL

The Panama Canal is the chief American contribution to Global War: Without it, the American continent would remain an unsurmountable obstacle to the (reasonable) rapid concentration of warships in either major ocean. Whereas the Suez Canal was conceived as a work of peace, the Panama Canal was primarily a military undertaking, intended to double the strength of the American fleet by allowing it to fight in both oceans.

To the other peoples who, from the year 1519 when Balboa (not Cortez) stood "silent upon a peak in Darien" and "gazed at the Pacific," the cutting-through of one of the three American isthmuses, Tuhuantepec, Nicaragua or Panama (the Isthmian Canal Commission published the proposed locations of nineteen different canal projects across Central America) was primarily another way of getting to the Far East.

For nearly a century, American strategists yearned for a canal. In 1880 President Rutherford B. Hayes announced grandiloquently that that Panamanian Isthmus was "part of the coastline of the United States." Yet a couple of years later not the Americans but the French started cutting a canal through part of this "American" coastline. They would have succeeded had they accepted the idea of a canal with locks rather than a sea-level channel, and had the world at the moment been able to deal with malaria and yellow fever. Nonetheless, the American achievement twenty years after the French failure was one of the greatest engineering successes ever recorded.

The Panama Canal is, including the maritime approach channels, nearly fifty miles long. A large part of it consists of Gatun Lake, kept in place by its gigantic Gatun Dam. The Isthmus just at this point twists like a worm. The inhabitants of Panama City see the sun rise in the east *over the Pacific* and set in the west over the Isthmus. Only the very largest ships cannot pass.

The annual tonnage has been somewhat less than that through Suez, and only about a third as much as that of Sault Sainte Marie on the Great Lakes. In 1938 American ships constituted thirty-two per cent of the total; of the American shipping, about two-thirds was between points on the American coasts.

The opening of the Panama Canal changed the commercial structure of the world. New Zealand and Vladivostok became nearer to Liverpool through Panama than through the Suez Canal. San Francisco became only a little further than New York from the tip of South Africa. The west coast of South America moved nearer to New York than to San Francisco—and was infinitely easier for the American Fleet to defend. The long, hard route around South America was almost deserted.

The problem of defending the United States changed radically. Part of it boiled down to holding the Panama Canal itself against attack or destruction. On the Atlantic side, the Canal is well defended by the bulk of Brazil and by the islands of the Caribbean. But in the Pacific it is decidedly exposed to attack overland or by airplanes operating from bases along the Pacific coast of South America. Foreign landings anywhere on the west coast of Central or South America had, if possible, to be prevented at almost any cost. The military tasks of the American forces were enormously extended.

Fortunately, the opening of the Canal made the accomplishing of these tasks possible—on condition that the Panama Canal itself was held, and held intact. For it compelled an enemy to face the total American fleet. Naval attack on the Pacific side of Panama became infinitely more difficult. Land-based planes ought—other things being equal—to prevent carrier-based enemy fighters or small bombers from getting through to bomb the Gatun Locks with any great volume or accuracy.

THE VITAL SHOULDER OF SOUTH AMERICA

Colombia, Venezuela, the Guianas, Brazil north of the Amazon jungles, are geographically part of South America, most of which faces east, but topographically they face north and front on the Caribbean. They are not only "unconnected" with the bulk of the continent to which they "belong," they are definitely separated from it by hundreds and hundreds of miles of jungle and swamp and wilderness without a railroad or even a decent road, where airfields are few and far between.

They therefore belong to the "lap" of the Americas and are infinitely "closer" to New York than to the inhabited portions of Brazil or to the Pacific countries like Ecuador—closer in time, in feeling, and in interests.

They and they alone form the section of South America which the United States must protect as part of its own defense—and which it *can* protect. South America "below the bulge" is as near to Europe as to the United States and could conceivably be occupied against American resistance, though without necessarily entailing the ultimate defeat of the United States.

Curiously enough, this "vital shoulder" is precisely the only region of South America upon which the United States is heavily dependent for vital materials.

To a German invader trained in *Geopolitik*, one natural invasion route of the Americas leads from West Africa across the 1500-mile-wide South Atlantic to the Brazilian Bulge at Recife and Natal—and could be taken by transport ships behind a barrier of warships well protected by fighters.

From Recife it is still two thousand miles to Port of Spain on Trinidad, the south sea gate to the Caribbean. Nearly a thousand miles' overland trek along the coast, at right angles to ranges of hills and several large rivers, would still bring the invaders only to Santa Maria de Belem (Para) on the south bank of the gigantic Amazon River—itself a formidable barrier. Belem is the depot of wild rubber from the Amazon Valley. From Belem to Port of Spain is a 1226-mile airline through jungle. Jungle is not the barrier we thought it, yet it is a safe bet that the Caribbean gate could only be taken by forces advancing over land, if they had previously annihilated or were able to keep the American air forces engaged elsewhere, in which case they would not need to advance by land. Command of the air would give them command of the sea, and by advancing slowly and establishing a series of air bases at fighter-plane-range intervals along the coast, they could eventually reach Trinidad, force its sea gate and enter the Caribbean.

In the process, they would have laid hands on Para rubber and the largest deposits of bauxite (aluminum ore) in the Western Hemisphere, located in British and Dutch Guiana. On Trinidad are not only oil wells but refineries where part of the inexhaustible oil of Venezuela is refined. The remainder is refined and stocked some five hundred miles to the westward, on the three little Dutch Islands called collectively Curaçao.

In time of major war, Guianan bauxite and Venezuelan oil are absolutely essential to the United States.

In short, unimpeded access to northern South America as far as Belem and beyond by sea and air is vital to American warfare. The taking-over and blocking of such routes by an invader would be a difficult but immensely profitable task.

Towns

Air line from the U.S.A. to Africa and the Middle and Far East
Sea route from the U.S.A. to Capetown and the Indian Ocean

Mountains: over 9000 feet / over 3000 feet

Even the presence of enemy submarines, able to refuel at any of the coastal ports or islands along the routes from Belem to Port of Spain and New York, could become an infernal nuisance. To eliminate it the United States might be compelled to take over all the "neutral spots" along the way for the duration.

THE WORST SEAWAY IN THE WORLD

Nature connected South America with Graham Land in Antarctica by a solid rock ridge but at the last moment forgot and left over six hundred miles of it under the sea. This is Drake Strait. Up to its discovery everyone believed the only passage from the Atlantic to the Pacific Ocean was the narrow Magellan Strait that separates Patagonia, the land of Big Feet, from the islands called collectively Tierra del Fuego. Therefore, the British kept the discovery of Drake Strait a secret and the honor of naming the southernmost point of South America went to a Dutchman, Le Maire, who, some thirty years later, called it after his home town, Cape Horn.

Cape Horn is—to sailors—the most famous promontory in the world because of its bleak rocks, freezing weather, tossing seas and howling gales.

Tierra del Fuego proper is divided between Argentina and Chile, but Magellan Strait passes through exclusively Chilean territory, from Cape Pilar on the west ("the stormiest headland known to seamen") to Cape of the Eleven Thousand Virgins on the Atlantic (actual length about 300 miles from ocean to ocean).

Ushuaia on Beagle Channel (between islands) is a sort of village capital. On the Atlantic side, the country is rather flat and practical for grazing; on the Chilean side, the islands are tops of sunken mountains, providing numerous deep fjords as in Norway and an archipelago surpassing in complexity anything found elsewhere on the planet. Unless sought from the air, considerable fleets could hide in a hundred places, unsuspected. Just to the north lies the "German" part of Chile.

Until the opening of the Panama Canal, the Patagonian straits were a very important route indeed and are still (virtually) the only sure sea passage between the two major oceans. The blocking or destruction of the Canal would again make them vital to the United States, the middle point of the thirteen-thousand-mile route between naval bases on the two American coasts. And since there are but two Trans-Andean railways (one is shown at the top of this map), the water road is also important for the defense of South America. With the Panama Canal open, it is considerably shorter from Cape Horn to New York via the Pacific than via the Atlantic. By other routes these Straits are about the same distance from the United States as from France and far closer to the west coast of Africa.

On the Atlantic side, the Straits are dominated by the British-owned Falkland Islands (with the lesser islands known as the Falkland Island Dependency—not shown here) and Graham Land in Antarctica. Before the war, the military value of these possessions was virtually nil. But existing scouting planes with twelve to fifteen hundred miles' radius operating from various British bases could keep the three passages (Magellan Strait, Beagle Strait and Drake Strait) under constant observation (in decent weather!) and bombers could sink the ships before they could land. On the other hand, a Chile that fell into Axis hands by invasion or insurrection, aided by an Argentine Republic committed to "playing safe," could make of the southern tip of South America a military bastion and air base and the center of eventual parachutist attacks that might take over the British possessions without too great difficulty. Passage of United Nations shipping would be possible only in the mildest weather.

Conclusion: the strategic importance of the inter-oceanic passages here is largely potential, but potentially large.

See also pages 59 and 119.

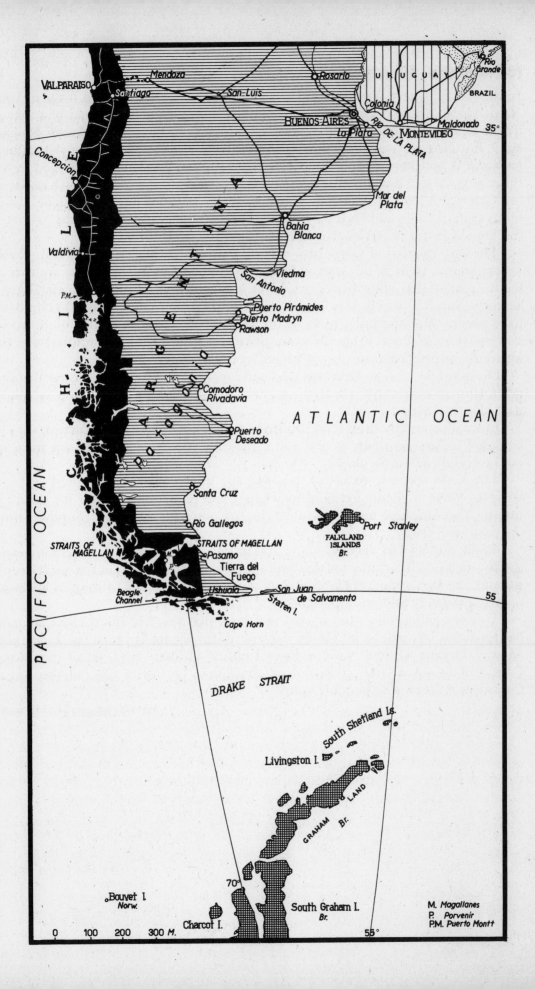

FROM ARCTIC TO ATLANTIC

In the North, where the Atlantic Ocean is pinched together before it opens into the Arctic Ocean, there is an all-year belt of open water. Close to Iceland you may come a cropper on an iceberg, and the same holds true for a thousand miles off Newfoundland. But Norway waters—thanks to the Gulf Stream—are relatively clear almost as far north as Spitzbergen. In winter Greenland is often joined to Spitzbergen by a solid sheet of pack ice. But on its southern tip and western side as far north as Godthab the Greenland coast remains fairly open and the winter temperature is no more rigorous than in Fargo and Duluth. In summer—fog permitting—air and sea passage from the United States to Soviet Russia is entirely practical.

The eastern coast of Greenland is for the most part high and forbidding and the ice cap pushes right to the sea and falls over towering cliffs. But there are two settlements, potential landing places, whatever you wish to call them—Angmagssalik and Scoresby Sund. Troop-carrier planes that could be serviced at Scoresby Sund would have a mere thousand miles to fly before taking Narvik—approximately the same distance as from Iceland. From the same place materials could be rapidly conveyed by air to the British Isles, in case of urgent need.

Or, in reverse action, Germans who had captured Britain or by-passed Britain and taken Iceland, might equip Scoresby Sund and Angmagssalik with supply stations, and use them for stepping stones.

In summer supply ships could go from the United States to Murmansk via Greenland and Iceland and only at one point, theoretically, have to come out from under the protection of battle planes.

The little volcanic island of Jan Mayen, just over three hundred miles from Scoresby Sund, is commonly used by whalers and offers some shelter for ships. As an intermediate seaplane base, it would bring its possessor within six hundred miles of the coast of Norway.

As the present war develops more and more into a gigantic struggle for control of the air, each side struggling for that prerequisite to advance on land or sea, Greenland, Iceland, the Shetlands and Faroes strung out between the two continents are strategic points of the very highest importance.

A mere civilian may even hazard the guess that some of the decisive sea and air battles of this war will be fought for control of the passage between the Arctic and the Atlantic Oceans. United Nations control means ultimate invasion of the European Continent by them; Axis control once established permits a blow at the American Continent at its most vulnerable point.

See also pages 51, 117 and 119.

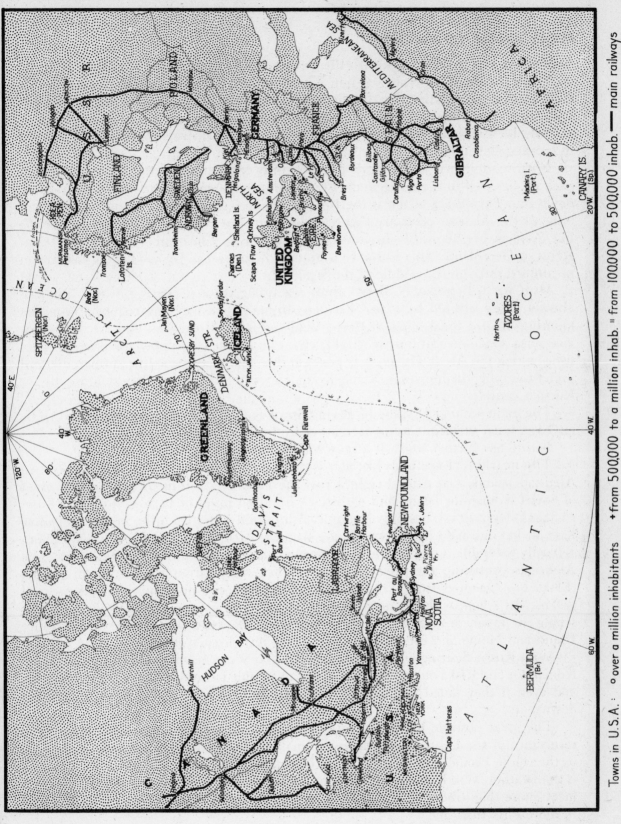

Towns in U.S.A. :   ° over a million inhabitants   + from 500,000 to a million inhab.   '' from 100,000 to 500,000 inhab.   — main railways

A   Anvers   Le H Le Havre   St N St. Nazaire
Ch °Cherbourg   MB Murray Bay (La Malbaie)

O Ostende
P Portsmouth

FROM ARCTIC TO PACIFIC

Connecting the Arctic Ocean with the Bering Sea and the Pacific is Bering Strait. It is 56 miles across at the nearest point. Therefore it has always been more of a bridge than a barrier. It was this way that the ancestors of the American Indians presumably came over from Asia not such a terribly long time ago.

The Russian explorers who took possession of Alaska had no difficulty whatever in crossing Bering Strait.

Narrow though it is the Strait is closed only in winter and the summer limit of pack ice lies well to the north and east. In summer dangerous drift ice is found well down into Bering Sea as far as the tip of Russian Kamchatka. This means that not only all the Alaskan ports are theoretically open but that Canadian Arctic harbors like Aklavik are accessible for several months, as is conceivably the passage clear across to Greenland. This is due to a branch of the warm Japan current that passes northward through the middle of the Strait.

Drift ice will probably always limit sea traffic through Bering Strait, but it is already being utilized by a few Russian ships that pass during the brief summer months with ice breaker escort, from Vladivostok to Murmansk and Archangel, or vice versa. Once the (all but) inevitable chain of properly equipped air bases is established along the Arctic Ocean, it is possible that Siberian towns like Ambarchik will prefer to supply themselves in Nome, Kodiak or even Sitka rather than in more distant Russian centers.

The main strategical value of Bering Strait is, indeed, giving sea access to Arctic air bases until such time as air freighters are built to bring everything needed.

Bering Sea further south is a center of problems of a different sort.

This nearly enclosed body of water is limited to the south by the American-owned Aleutian Islands that extend right across the Pacific to within three hundred miles of Soviet Komandor Island and within six hundred miles of Petropavlovsk on Kamchatka. Petropavlovsk lies only a couple of hundred miles from the nearest Japanese base on Paramushiro Island, last of the Kuriles. Attu, the furthest of the Aleutians, is hardly habitable. Last American outpost was, at the beginning of 1942, Kiska. The Aleutians constitute the greatest existing offensive position against Japan proper (Kiska is 2000 miles from Tokyo)—but only if well equipped for both offense and defense. In a fight with Japan, without Russian participation, the United States risk seeing the Japanese sneak a fleet northward on the Russian side to seize St. Lawrence Island and Nome and come down on the southern coast from behind.

With Russia fighting on the side of the United States, naval patrols operating from Komandor and Kiska ought, between them, to be able to head off any such expedition, and even if they failed in this, to enable Russo-American air forces to isolate and destroy it.

The great obstacle to any operations in this north country—which explains the reluctance of the United States forces to make the Aleutian Islands that "key point to the whole Pacific" which air-minded General "Billy" Mitchell said it should be—is the weather. Winds are terrific and fogs, formed where the warm and cold currents meet, more than frequent. Air operations from the Aleutians are bound to be costly in more ways than one.

See also page 107.

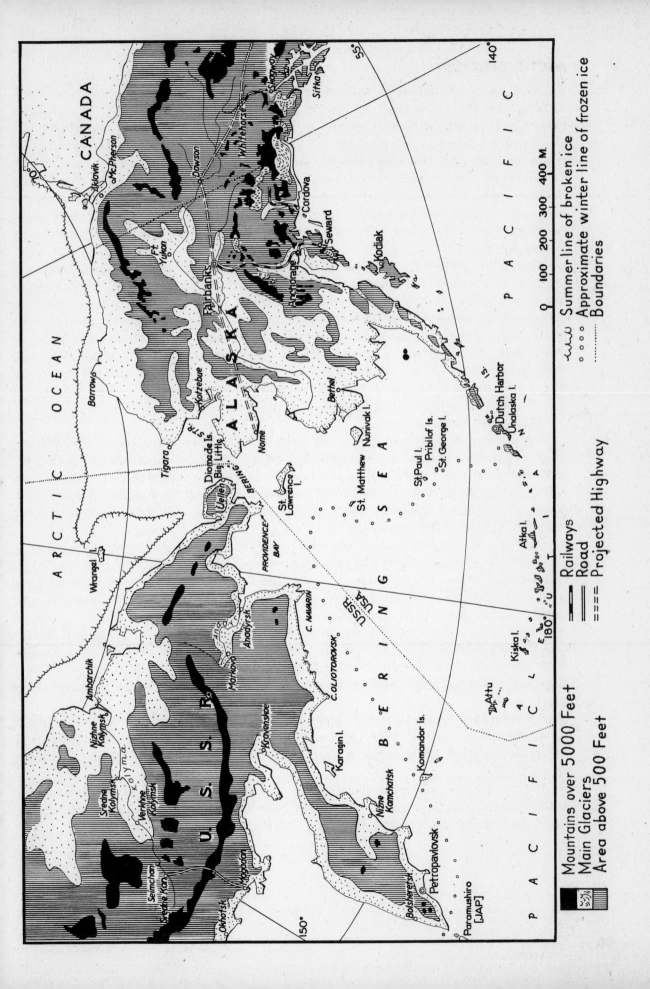

ARCTIC STRATEGY

Much of the earth's habitable land and most of the earth's people are in the Northern Hemisphere. Only one large continent, South America, is largely in the Southern Hemisphere. It might be maintained without paradox that little of importance has yet happened south of the Equator. Obviously, this may mean that South America is the territory that promises most for the future.

The center of the Northern Hemisphere is the Arctic Ocean, with the North Pole in the middle. The Arctic Ocean is really a sort of inland sea. Like the Mediterranean, it has two outlets—one nine hundred miles across into the Atlantic between Norway and Greenland, the other only thirty-six miles across into the Pacific, known as Bering Strait.

One good reason why this inland sea did not, like the Mediterranean, become a center of civilization (and a German Nazi geographer, Hermann Wirth, traces the rise of civilization to "Nordics" who came into Europe from Greenland) lies in the fact that lots of the Arctic Ocean are frozen over most of the time, and nearly all of it some of the time. The chief exception is along the Norwegian and Russian coast as far as Murmansk, the "original" sea gate to Russia, where flows the last trickle of the warm Gulf Stream. In fact, since the last Tropical Age, men seem to have avoided the Arctic Ocean and its adjacent coasts as much as possible. Not only was it cold but people found it hard to adjust to a rhythm of six months' sleep and six months' waking.

All this has changed.

On the sea, the Russians, who never seem to know when it is too cold for comfort, gradually discovered that with ice-breaker escort, for about four months each year they could get ships right across their northern coastal waters from Archangel to Uellen, Petropavlovsk and Vladivostok, and did so. Then they managed to develop towns on rivers and inlets far north of the Arctic Circle and induce people to stay in them without police persuasion.

Yet the real Arctic revolution was brought by the airplane. For at 36,000 feet where the bombers now fly and the new passenger and freight planes will fly, it is not appreciably colder over the North Pole than over the Equator. Supplies to Russia, supplies to Norway, perhaps, can travel across quiet frozen regions in huge air freighters conceivably larger than any existing planes. Via the Pole, Los Angeles is closer to Moscow than to Rio de Janeiro, Detroit nearer to Narvik than Norfolk, Virginia, and Seattle only a trifle farther. The shortest air route from New York or Boston to Manila leads across the Arctic Ocean, Siberia, Manchuria and the China Sea! Sooner or later bombers and giant freight and passenger planes will make it that way, in about three hops.

Already Axis ships and fighter planes are trying to intercept United Nations aid to Russia via Murmansk. Were Murmansk lost, they would have even more reason for trying to cut off aid from North America coming to some other Russian or Chinese center by air.

Were Japan to isolate the Russian Far East by cutting the Trans-Siberian Railroad at some point well inland, the Soviet authorities would certainly try to supplement their summer ship route along the Arctic coast by all-year air traffic.

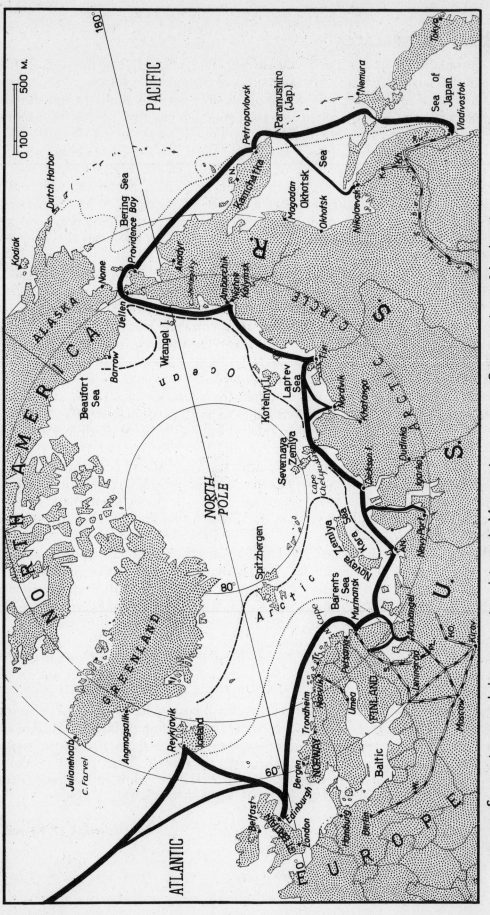

Sea route open whole year eastward towards Murmansk and 2 to 3 months per year eastward from Murmansk.

Railways

━━━ Summer line of broken ice

┄┄┄ Winter sea freezing line

AN Andierma
K Komsomolsk.

Kh Khabarovsk
N Nizhne Kamchatsk

KO Kotlas
PL Plesetskaya

S Sorotskaya
Tr Tromsö

W Warsaw

THE STRAIT OF MALACCA

Of all the seaways from the Pacific Ocean into the Indian Ocean through that mass of East Indian islands that identify themselves so patently as a sunken continent, none was so famous or important as the Strait of Malacca between Sumatra and the Malay Peninsula, with the British-owned, mostly Chinese-populated port of Singapore. If you headed around the Cape of Good Hope, you might prefer Sunda Strait, the narrow channel between Sumatra and Java. But if you came from or were going to India or Europe—and most shipping in time of peace did—then the Malacca Strait was your pathway. It was safer and more practical than any other. Strategically, it was safe against all but amphibian attack under a canopy of airplanes. When, more than a century ago, the great Raffles traded back captured Java to the Netherlands for a tiny island at the end of the Malay Peninsula, few thought him wise. But the intervening years have proved him right.

Singapore was the key to the East Indies and the China Sea. The Japanese *blitz* capture of Singapore was not only a death blow to traditional sea-power theories, but gave them real entrance into the Indian Ocean through the Malacca Strait.

On its eastern end, the Malacca Strait gives entrance, through tiny islands countless as pepper grains on meat, to the China Sea. On the west, the Strait offers shelter for a fleet that, protected by superior aircraft, can take possession of the Bay of Bengal and strike at Ceylon, the key to the Indian Ocean.

Development of air power has modified the character of warfare in amphibian regions like this more than elsewhere. But so long as troops, supplies, heavy war materials are still transported by ship, just so long will the Malacca Strait remain a principal corridor. With this Strait in enemy hands, British and Dutch possessions short of Australia were doomed to occupation and Australia to permanent danger.

Without possession of the Strait, Japanese conquests on both sides of the China Sea were precarious and conceivably ephemeral. With the Strait firmly back in United Nations hands, Japan would be well on the way to losing the war, almost regardless of its conquests elsewhere.

Britain, the Netherlands and the United States lost their East Indian possessions partly from lack of preparation, but even more through faulty preparation—the failure to realize how fully territory of this sort lends itself to three-dimensional air, water and land warfare carefully co-ordinated. Recovery of the Malacca Strait would be the first necessary step in saving India and recuperating a lost initiative.

Further East, between Australian Cape York and New Guinea is Torres Strait. It was discovered by Luis Vas de Torres in 1608 and considered so valuable that it was kept secret by the Spaniards and "rediscovered" by the great Cook in 1770. Nominally, this strait is 115 miles wide but, in the words of *La Grande Encyclopédie,* "it is to such an extent littered with coral reefs, shoals, shallows and little islands that maritime insurance companies refuse to insure ships passing through it." I doubt this, for in time of peace a regular line of steamships went from Batavia to Brisbane through Prince of Wales Channel in Torres Strait. But the Strait is bad enough and to the east lies the Great Barrier Reef—a horror to sailors—while the western entrance to the Strait from the Arafura Sea is nearly blocked by coral.

See also pages 17, 73 and 105.

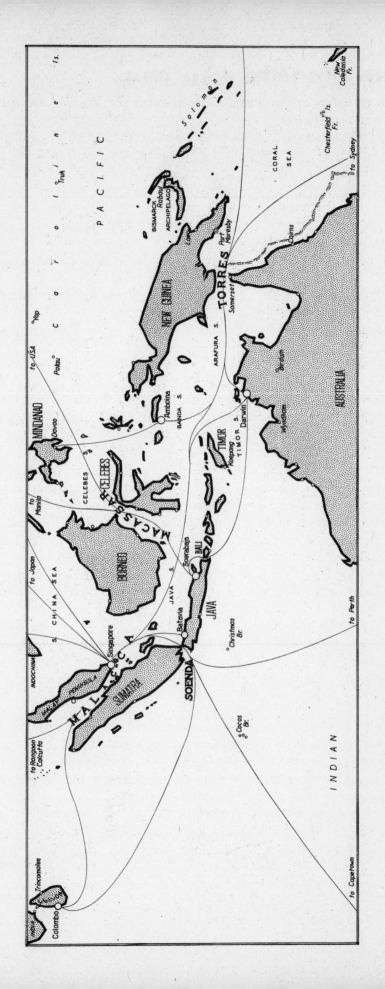

SOUTHERN GATES TO THE INDIAN OCEAN

Of the many gates to the Indian Ocean from the Pacific, the three most southern lie in Australian waters.

The southernmost is probably the best—and it is not a gate at all, but an open passage a thousand miles and more in breadth between the New Zealand Islands and the bit of French-owned Antarctica called Adélie Land. Here, as long as you keep north of the limit of drift ice, navigation is reasonably safe.

Going into the Pacific through the Coral Sea and the Tasman Sea, when you leave the eastern ports of Australia—Brisbane and Sydney—you can navigate pretty freely toward the two Americas.

But if your path is around Australia you are tempted to seek passage through one of two very bad channels.

Torres Strait (see page 52) with Timor Strait between Timor and Australian Darwin is a route navigators avoid when they can.

Bass Strait, between Australia and Tasmania, where ships from Sydney (Australian naval base) pass to and fro on their way to Africa and Europe, is not very much more hospitable to navigators. It is about 138 miles wide, with ten to twelve foot tides, wild currents running three or four miles an hour, coral reefs and wicked little islands.

Between Torres Strait and Bass Strait lies most of what is valuable in Australia and one may say that nature has protected Australia well against sea attack from the west. Warships operating from Sydney and land-based planes should be able totally to close Bass Strait.

Their heaviest task might turn out to be the protection of the New Zealand Islands several hundred miles away. One might expect an amphibian enemy operating in three dimensions to avoid Torres Strait altogether and, from New Guinea southeastward, to use the Solomon Islands, the New Hebrides, the Fijis and New Caledonia as stepping stones to New Zealand, in an effort to isolate Australia from the Americas before attacking it.

The first Japanese attack in the Coral Sea seemed to fortify this thesis. The worst thing about strategy is that the enemy often knows what you know and knows it better.

See also pages 107 and 109.

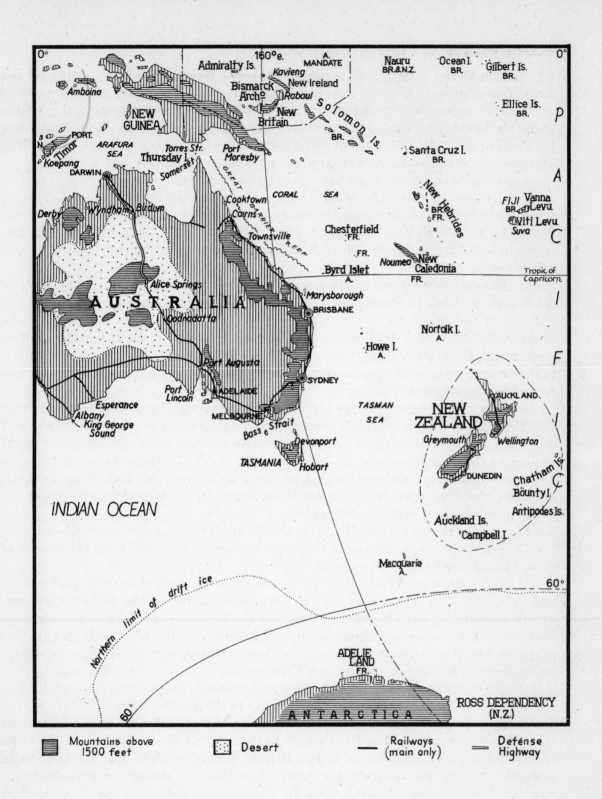

GOING PLACES ON THE INDIAN OCEAN

The Indian Ocean is hardly an ocean at all; just a tremendous bay opening off the Antarctic, which is itself hardly an ocean but just a name given to the southern sections of the other oceans contiguous to the Antarctic Continent. Considering the Indian Ocean as merely the piece of water between the Cape of Good Hope and Cape Leeuwen in Australia and north of a line connecting them, it is still a tidy piece. From Capetown to Freemantle, Australia, is 4711 sea miles. From the line connecting the two to the top of the tremendous bay, say to Karachi in India, is over 4000 sea miles.

This "ocean" is bounded on the west by Africa and the thousand-mile-long coast of Arabia called the Hadhramaut, on the east by Burma and Thailand and the Malay Peninsula, the Dutch East Indies and Australia. At the top (the north) it forks into two—the Arabian Sea and the Bay of Bengal, with, between them, the steaming peninsula of India.

In the northwest corner are two water pockets with holes in them, the Gulf of Aden and the Gulf of Oman; the one hole leads to the Red Sea and through the Suez Canal to Europe, the other to the Persian Gulf, which gives on Iraq and the roads to the Black Sea, the Dardanelles and Soviet Russia. From either the Gulf of Aden or the Gulf of Oman northwest to the North Sea is the shortest and most practical line along which to cut the land-mass of Europe-Asia-Africa neatly in two and dominate it strategically.

In the northeast corner, at the top of the Bay of Bengal, start the overland roads to China, bad roads but the only ones there are. Between the Malay mainland and the Indies and Australia to the east, are three main passages (among many minor ones) leading to the China Sea; the Strait of Malacca; the Timor Sea-Arafura Sea-Torres Strait into the Coral Sea that is part of the Pacific; and the Bass Strait between Australia and Tasmania. South of this is the open Antarctic beckoning around the world (provided you miss the icebergs).

The Indian Ocean was Sindbad the Sailor's playground. It is essentially a center from which to go places. Because you can go so many places, this body of water is of great strategic importance in a global war.

At the beginning of World War Two, practically all of the strategical points here, and most of the many scattered islands, were in the hands of the British Commonwealth of Nations. British was Capetown at the south tip of Africa; British were Berbera and Aden commanding the Red Sea entrance; British, to all intents and purposes, the Arabian side of the Persian Gulf; British was India with the dominating bases at Bombay, Colombo and Trincomalee in Ceylon; British was Singapore and Australia. Other strategic points were either Dutch (to the east) or French. The Netherlands Indies guarded the minor passages to the Pacific. French Djibuti shared dominion over the Red Sea passage and French Madagascar with its naval base at Diego Suarez was a fine place from which to threaten all the traffic around the Cape of Good Hope. Yet so long as a non-British "intruder" into the Indian Ocean grabbed bases on only one side, sea traffic could proceed, though adventurously. If, however, it seized bases on both sides, or worse, successfully snatched Ceylon, then the Indian Ocean would be transformed from a vast network of British sea lanes into a theater of air and naval warfare—and not much else. A superior enemy fleet operating from Indian Ocean bases would split the British Commonwealth wide open.

See also page 67.

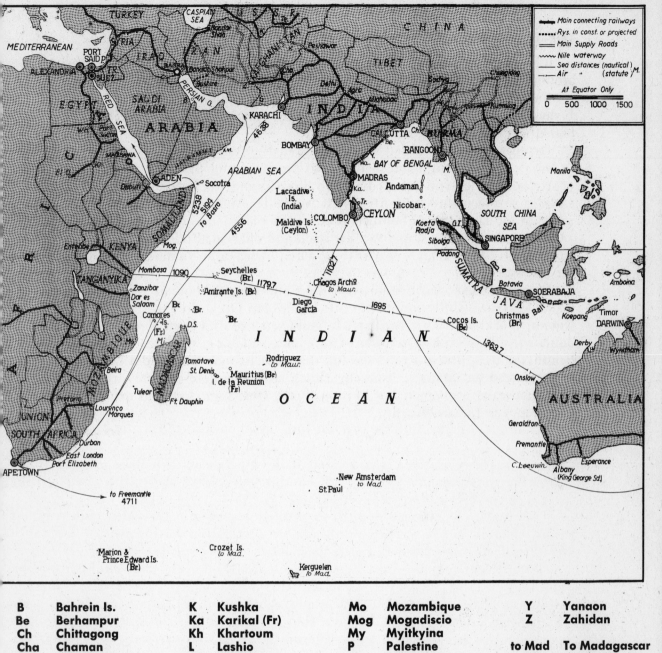

Short of this, the British positions in the Indian Ocean would have to be "flanked" by land operations, presumably in the northwest and northeast corner countries, and aiming at India. These corners would have to be overcome. Germans in the Arabian Sea plus Japanese in the Bay of Bengal would have denatured the ocean, almost regardless of how many island bases the British Commonwealth was able to hold on to. Communications between South Africa and Australia, or between the South Atlantic and the South Pacific, would move into the Antarctic or cease to be.

THE EASY PASSAGE AROUND AFRICA

Africa was the last continent to be penetrated and explored, but the sea route around it is the easiest inter-oceanic passage on earth.

Cape Horn is a sailors' nightmare but all seafarers love the Cape of Good Hope. It does not extend down unreasonably toward Antarctica—like Cape Horn. It is not frozen or gale-swept or forbidding.

Capetown might be called "centrally located"; from there it is less than 4500 miles to Rio de Janeiro and Natal in Brazil, to Freetown and Bathurst on the West Coast of Africa, to Aden and the Red Sea; to Karachi and the Persian Gulf; to Colombo, Ceylon; to Freemantle and Albany in Australia. And 4500 miles is just about the range of the latest-model bomber or transport plane.

The approaches to Capetown are open and offer small cover for lurking submarines. There are no islands nearby to be seized by sea or air raiders and made bases for easy air attack.

From old Diaz who first reached the Cape from Lisbon in 1488 and Vasca da Gama who successfully rounded it into the Indian Ocean in 1497, to the Americans, who, in World War Two, regularly brought war material from New York and Philadelphia to a Red Sea base, navigators have always found it, of all sea voyages of similar length, the most pleasant in peace and the safest in war. No wonder that the British early insisted on taking it from the Dutch and have kept it as a part of a British Commonwealth ever since. For in time of war, with Suez closed, its owner has a half-nelson on the Indian Ocean.

See also page 45.

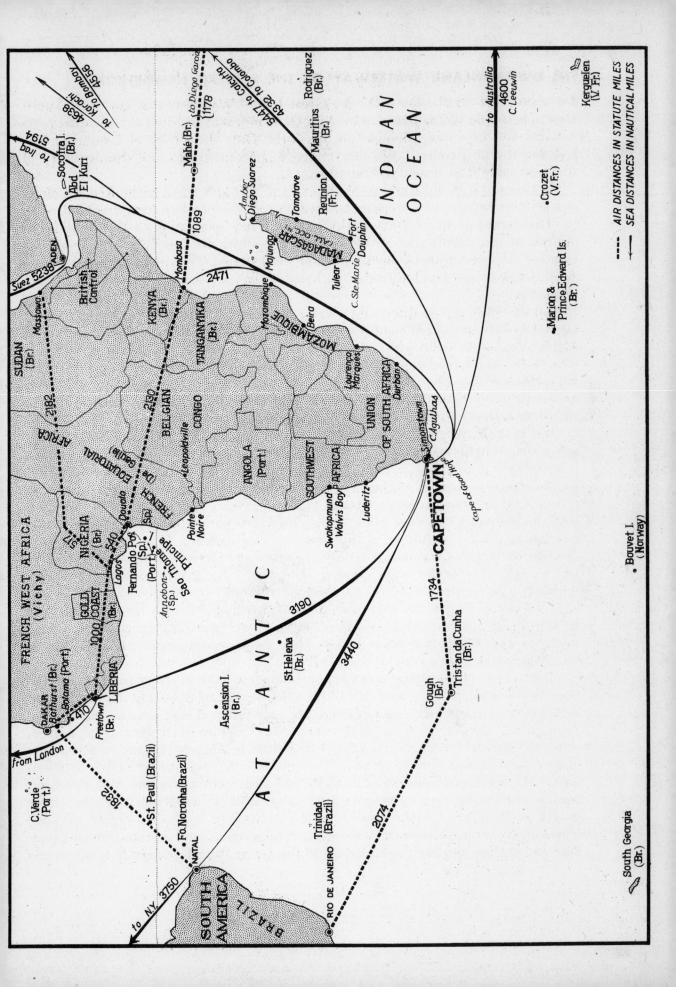

THE GREAT INLAND WATERWAY OF THE EASTERN HEMISPHERE

For 2500 years—until 1492 A.D.—the Great Inland Waterway that cuts the Eastern Hemisphere (the World Island of modern German professors) into two unequal parts was the most important highroad in the world. Only the seizure of Constantinople and Suez by unfriendly Turks determined to prevent traffic, and the discovery of America made it of secondary importance.

In Classical days one could go by ship up the Nile and across to the Red Sea along a canal built by Darius the Persian. It silted up and was forgotten for a thousand years.

That world declined. In the Middle Ages a new generation of Italian seafarers again made the Mediterranean the main link between the east and the west. Pisan, Genoese, Venetian galleys plied back and forth between Egypt and Italy, between Black Sea ports and London Bridge, exchanging the products of Europe for the riches of the East.

All this time the Mediterranean was a commercial link, but a strategic barrier. Gradually Britain secured control of the strategic points and erected bases. Gibraltar, Malta, Alexandria—with sea power and sea power alone, they could be maintained. They were maintained—against Napoleon, against the Germans in 1914. For meanwhile the Suez Canal had been opened and the Great Inland Waterway extended 1608 miles further to the Gulf of Aden and the Indian Ocean. With this entire passage in British or friendly hands, the all-red Empire was reasonably safe.

But in the Nineteenth Century Spain, France and Italy acquired North African territories, roughly across the sea from their homelands. They thus came into a position to cut British communications through the sea by their own transversal communications. For the Mediterranean is roughly five times as long as it is wide. It is divided into two parts by the Italian Peninsula, Sicily and Malta. From Gibraltar to Malta is about a thousand miles. Across the widest part, from Marseille or Toulon to Oran or Algiers or Bizerte, is just over half that distance. From French Oran to the Spanish base at Cartagena it is only 115 miles and Oran is an admirable place in which to lie in wait for ships entering or leaving the Mediterranean. Thus it is normally much easier to keep the shorter north-south routes open than the longer west-east route. Under any circumstances it is dubious if British connections could be kept open were two Mediterranean Powers to be bent on cutting them. Which might explain the British haste in attacking the (possibly hostile) French fleet in Oran Harbor in July 1940.

The advent of air power still further endangered the longitudinal communications. It was soon demonstrated that to keep the west route open and the north-south routes closed, would take overwhelming air superiority. The Germans and Italians "neutralized" Malta by repeated bombardment, and sneaked their own convoys across to Libya with comparative ease. British ships in Alexandria were in permanent danger. So, too, were Italian ships at Taranto, but that was cold comfort. In short, with Italo-Germans in possession of Sicily and Crete and Libya, the Mediterranean became just another river—a broader Amazon or Mississippi extending, with adjacent waters, almost four thousand miles from the Atlantic to the Indian Ocean. As such it remained a strategic obstacle of the highest importance, and a protection to Egypt, Suez and the coveted Middle East. Loss of the Great Inland Waterway to an enemy strong on land and possessing superior or equal air power would mean this enemy's expansion over most of the Eastern Hemisphere. On the other hand, overwhelmingly superior air power would enable the United Nations to clear the Inland Waterway of enemy shipping, destroy enemy war fleets, and at the time and place of choice, invade Axis-dominated Europe on its "soft" southern side.

The Strait of Gibraltar

The Strait of Gibraltar, with the unequal Pillars of Hercules on either side, was the theoretical limit of the Classical World and beyond it lay the eschatological Islands of the Blessed. Practical, hardy Phoenician navigators in swift galleys passed through on the way to Cornish tin mines at least as early as 600 B.C., and there is evidence of their reaching the Cape of Good Hope at approximately the same time (see Herodotus: *Melpomene*). On the south stand the rough hills of Morocco, on the north, the rugged Sierra Nevada of Southern Spain and the Rock of Gibraltar itself. This latter "pebble" rises to about 1400 feet above sea level and was, until the development of air power and the super-bomb, the strongest fortress in the world. Even today its labyrinthine tunnels and galleries could not be blasted out as Corregidor was blasted; but its well-equipped harbor could be rendered unfit for any shipping, if not utterly destroyed. Without supporting ships or planes, the Rock would remain a fortified pin-point on a channel barely nine miles wide whose traffic it could not, at least at night, expect to stop or impede. Nonetheless, the Rock remains one of the strategical king spots of the world.

The Strait itself is over 1300 feet deep and traversed by a steady inward flowing current. Ceuta, the "little pillar" on the African side, is not so spectacular as the Rock, but its very lowness gives it great advantages for modern warfare by offering far less target with almost equal shelter and closer proximity to adequate airfields.

Within the Mediterranean, on the African coast, are three good French naval and air bases: Oran (Mers-el-Kabir), Algiers and Bizerte, this last rivalling Malta itself as a bulwark, splitting the Mediterranean in two at its narrowest place.

The Suez Canal

Had the Suez Canal been open in 1492, America might not have been discovered for a century. Nobody in Europe wanted to go to America. What they really wanted to reach was the gold of "Ophir" (possibly in Sumatra) and the islands whence came the strong-tasting spice that enabled men not to gag at unrefrigerated meat.

The modern Suez Canal was finished in 1869 by a Frenchman, Ferdinand de Lesseps, after fifteen years of digging. It belongs in law to an international company but is controlled by Great Britain. It is, with its sea approaches, about a hundred and nine miles long.

As a link in the Great Inland Waterway across the World Island (Europe-Asia-Africa) of the German "geopoliticians," joining the Mediterranean and North Atlantic with the Red Sea, the Indian Ocean, and ultimately with the Pacific, its strategic importance is immense. The route from Liverpool through the Suez Canal is notably shorter than the one around the Cape of Good Hope—4457 miles shorter to Bombay,

3323 to Yokohama, 872 miles shorter to Melbourne. In 1937, 6635 ships carrying 697,800 passengers and over thirty-four million tons of freight paid passage tolls to the Company.

Physically, it is a long ditch linking three continents. Most of it was dug in soft sand and is kept open by constant dredging. There are no locks and it is hardly vulnerable to bombardment; sand displaced can be quickly and easily removed. To the eastward a railroad leads into Palestine and either to Europe or to Basra on the Persian Gulf. Planes and railroads might displace the Canal as a passenger route; planes and trains and trucks might carry expensive freight more rapidly and cheaply. Pipe lines could move the oil of Mesopotamia and Iran. But as a military and heavy-draught highway, the Suez Canal remains one of the vital communications of the world.

But only so long as the Inland Waterway—Mediterranean-Canal-Red Sea—can be kept open. Even with the British holding Gibraltar, Malta, Alexandria, Suez, Port Said and Aden a single large Mediterranean country on the side of or occupied by the enemy could keep it passable for convoys of merchant ships or transports only by vastly superior air power supplementing naval control. Without such air power, the inland-sea route across the World Island would cease to be a route and become merely a barrier to further advance on either side.

The Red Sea and the Gulf of Aden

Of the Red Sea the most that can be said is that it is fifteen hundred miles long, hot, steamy and not very deep; keeping a dry passage across the bottom for the Children of Israel to leave Egypt and pass over on foot was relatively easy for the Almighty.

Humanly, the most interesting town on the Red Sea is Jidda, the port of Mecca, where in normal times debark those thousands of pious Moslem pilgrims who spend the money that keeps Saudi Arabia going. Politically, the center of interest is Massawa in Italian Eritrea. It was from here that Mussolini sent his men and material up into nearby Ethiopia on one of the most misguided adventures of all times. And it is at Massawa that in 1941 the Americans started widening out a base for the supply of the United Nations armies operating in the zone centering in the Suez Canal.

French Djibuti and British Aden control the Strait and the Gulf of Aden. British Zeila and Berbera and Italian Alula are third-rate ports. Djibuti could be seized from the French at any time, but consideration for Vichy still prevented the operation.

The Straits of Bab El Mandeb normally form one of the great gateways of the world. But with the Mediterranean virtually closed, the Red Sea and the Gulf of Aden are reduced to being a sort of giant outer harbor for powers operating in the Middle Eastern war zone, and a second line to be bitterly defended should the Suez Canal be captured.

See also pages 11, 23, 95 and 97.

1 Port Etienne
2 Villa Cisneros
3 Agadir
4 Mogador
5 Mazagan
6 Rabat
7 Melila
8 Cartagena
9 Philippeville
10 Bone
11 Susa
12 Gabès
13 Palma
14 Marseille
15 Cagliari
16 Trapani
17 Palermo
18 Catania
19 Brindisi
20 Valona
21 Derna
22 Sollum
23 Aqaba
24 Jaffa
25 Beirut
26 Burgas
27 Varna
28 Constanta
29 Novorossiisk
30 Poti
31 Batum
32 Trabzon
33 Samsun
34 Astrakhan
35 Baku
36 Bandar Shahpur
37 Tehran
T Tunis

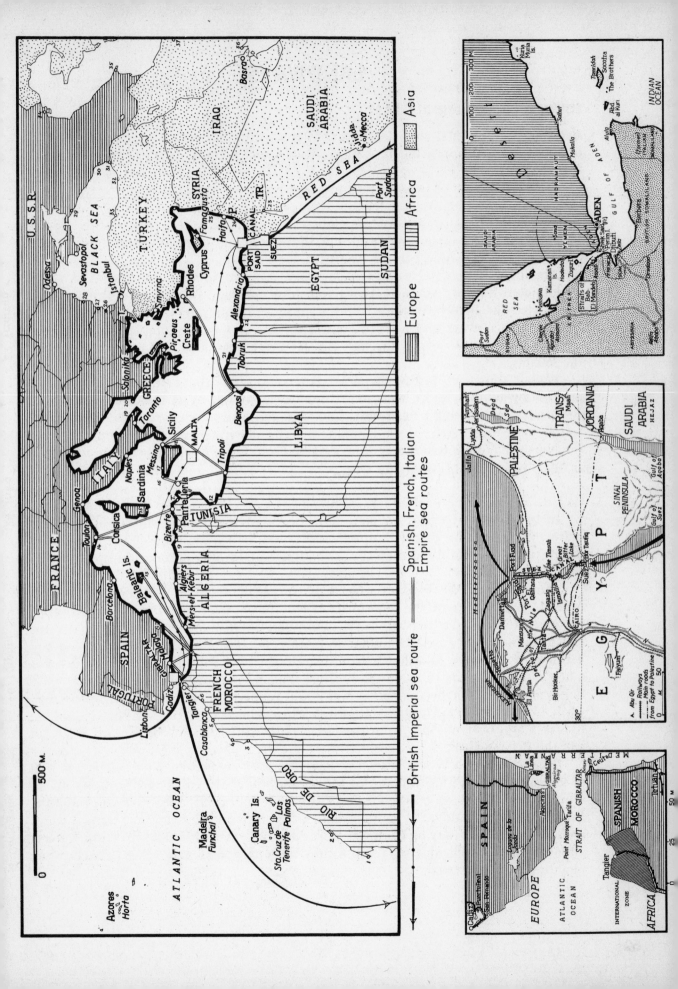

Europe

Africa

Asia

British Imperial sea route

Spanish, French, Italian
Empire sea routes

LANDWAYS

EUROPE TO THE MIDDLE EAST

Back in 1904 Sir Halford Mackinder, after meditating upon the countless migratory peoples first appearing in Eastern Russia and Central Asia, gave a lecture in London entitled *The Geographical Pivot of History*. His thesis was world history has been the result of peoples pushing outward from the continental center upon "peripheral" peoples. Mackinder saw Europe, Asia and Africa as a single unit, the World Island. Nine-twelfths of the globe, he noted, are water; two-twelfths are the World Island; the remaining twelfth is the rest of the land. One scattered twelfth cannot oppose two concentrated twelfths.

About the same time, some Germans had come to another conclusion: in order to dominate Europe, Asia and Africa you must cut them in two! Now this was precisely what the British, in their blind amphibian instinct, had accomplished during the previous century and a half. They had, that is, secured complete control over the Great Inland Waterway through the Mediterranean and Red Seas to India and the Pacific.

Back in those days before air power, you could only drive a fleet out of a strategic position by another better fleet—something Germany was in no position to build, for Britain had got too big a head start. But what you could do was to divide the World Island by a broad strip of land paralleling the maritime route and running from the North Sea to the Red Sea and the Persian Gulf. Once you had cut the water route at Suez, you could press on and take Africa on one hand and India on the other by superior land power. When Germans of this sort got control of the Reich, they began their *Drang nach Osten* and started laying a strategic railway from Berlin to Baghdad.

In 1914 they had a go at the main task—beating Great Britain and confiscating the better morsels of the British Empire—and failed by a neck. One of the reasons for failure was the inability of their Turkish allies to take Suez and cut the water route, according to the plan.

After the First World War, a German army geographer, Karl Haushofer, saw in Mackinder's writings on the superiority of land power over sea power the appropriate *leit-motiv* to bring Germany to world dominion. Germany was almost as well located as Russia (designated by Mackinder) to be the "heart land" of the World Island and get hold of the latter. Haushofer became an intimate of Adolf Hitler. The result was a new *Drang nach Osten* along the Berlin-Baghdad Railway, this time with far better hopes of success. For by 1939 air power could render the Mediterranean impassable, while in Italian Libya Germany possessed a bridgehead in Africa, making it possible to attack and overrun Suez from two sides, meanwhile pressing on toward Baghdad and the Persian Gulf.

Between the two World Wars, the Baghdad Railway had been completed, as well as several others. With unimportant boat trips, you could go by rail from Narvik in Norway to either Basra on the Persian Gulf or to Suez itself. Suez gave you the Nile. From Basra you could go by motor trucks across Iran and Baluchistan. Or you could go from Warsaw by way of Baku. Or from Moscow, take a Pullman to Tashkent and after one not too difficult trek, reach Kabul, with only the Khyber Pass between your plodding feet and India!

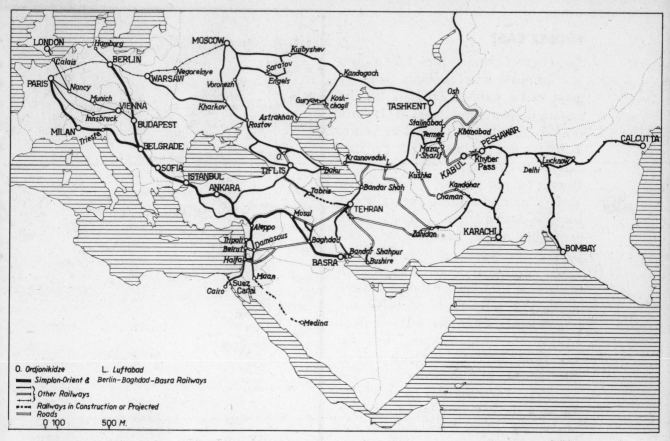

O. Ordjonikidze   L. Luftabad

▬▬▬ Simplon-Orient & Berlin-Baghdad-Basra Railways

≡≡≡ Other Railways

▪▪▪ Railways in Construction or Projected

--- Roads

0   100   500 M.

Motor cross-tracks linked up the railway through Syria with the Berlin-Baghdad line. Even the hard tracks of Arabia, it appeared, were perfectly navigable for motor vehicles properly equipped. At Baghdad you could—if you preferred—continue by road to Teheran, whence road and rail combine in an entirely feasible system of communications leading into Soviet Russia.

In short, modern scientific developments were granting advantage after advantage to a superior Continental land power, advantages of a type that not even Mackinder had dreamed. All you had to do was to eliminate powerful enemies from your flanks —and drive your wedge from the Atlantic to the Indian Ocean.

THE MIDDLE EAST TO THE FAR EAST

Global War requires thinking in continents. Increased communications demand increased imaginations. Modern battles are won by the fellow who gets there first with the most brain power.

The last years have seen an incredible increase in communications between the Far East and the Middle East. Twenty years ago you would have had to ride the Trans-Siberian, then walk or fly. Then the Russians built the Turkestan-Siberian Railway linking Siberia with Turkestan and Krasnovodsk on the Caspian, on the other side of which super saline sea you could catch another train for Odessa and Europe. Then the British lengthened the Indian Railways across Baluchistan to beyond Zahidan. And the Persians—pardon me, the Iranians—managed to get a line completed from the Persian Gulf to the Caspian at Bandar Shah. When the branch is completed from Teheran to Tabriz, you will be able to go by rail from Murmansk to

MIDDLE EAST

Kum near Teheran—then take a car a few hundred miles along a perfectly good motor road to Zahidan, hit the Indian Railways and travel to Calcutta or even to Sadiya or Imphal in Assam. You have not yet reached the Far East and between Imphal and Kalewa in Burma (where you hit a highway) or Yell (where you meet the railroad) there is nothing but a jungle track across one of the least favored countries in the world. British Colonials either because they loved steamships or because they feared Indian nationalism, just refused to establish any proper land connections between their Indian vice regency and Burma. Therefore they could not well send reinforcements to Burma once they lost Rangoon. The only way to attack India from the east may be by sea from Chittagong. From Thailand you can go by rail to Singapore or Hanoi.

Diversity of railway gauge does constitute an obstacle. Burma and Assam roads are mostly narrow gauge. Iranian Railways are European or standard gauge—four feet eight and a half inches. Most Indian railways are five feet six inches wide and the broadest in the world—six inches wider than Russian broad gauge. It means a lot of changing, but does not prevent traffic.

The meaning of all this is clear: should the Japanese take India and the Germans cross the Caucasus, they would be in a position to engage in a pincers drive around the *entire* Asiatic Continent, thus fulfilling the wildest deliriums of Pan-Germanists, Geopolitkers and *Hakko Ichi-u-ers*. Success in such an operation would go far toward making the Axis impregnable.

See also pages 53, 57, 95, 101 and 105.

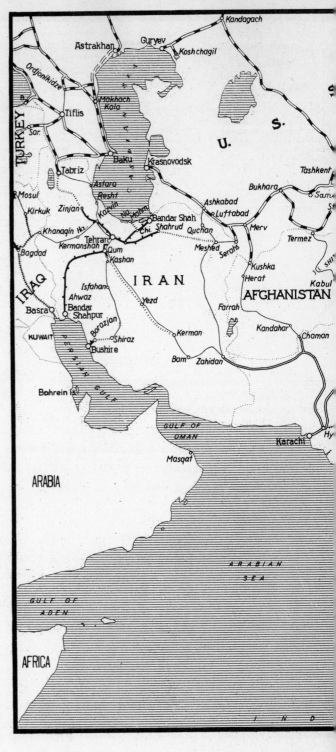

═══ Railways 5'6"gauge ⊶⊶⊶ Railways 5'0"ga

B	Batum	G	Gauhati
Ch	Chungtien	Gal	Galaghat (or
Cha	Chamutong		Galagunj)
Chi	Chirja	H	Hweili
FH	Fort Hertz (or	Ha	Hamadan
	Putao, Kandi,	Hg	Hangchow
	Khampti)	Ho	Hochih

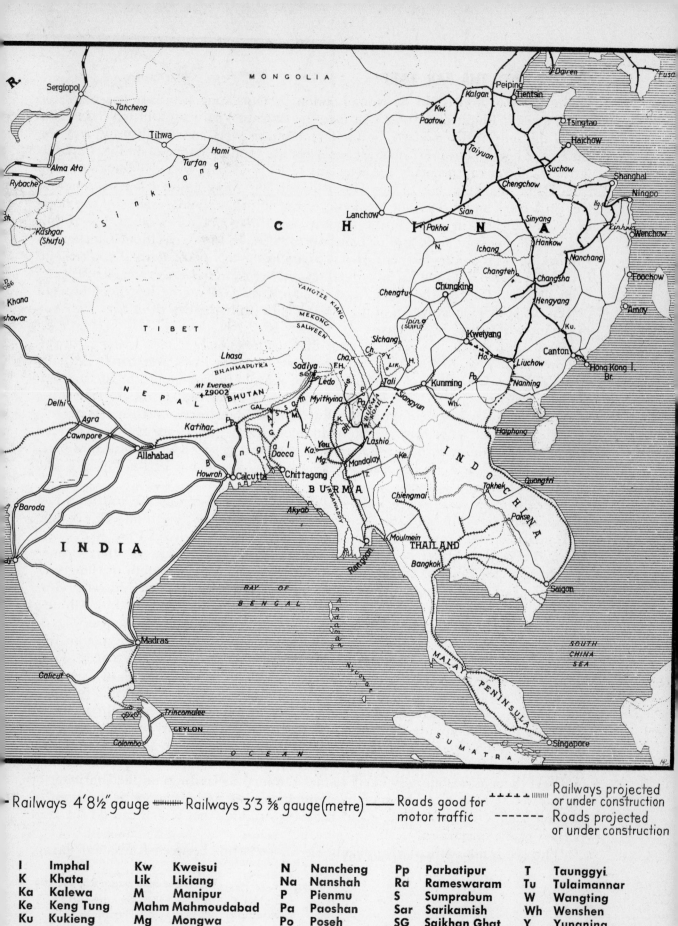

- Railways 4'8½" gauge   ++++++ Railways 3'3⅜" gauge (metre)   —— Roads good for motor traffic   ++++++++ Railways projected or under construction   - - - - - Roads projected or under construction

I	Imphal	Kw	Kweisui	N	Nancheng	Pp	Parbatipur	T	Taunggyi
K	Khata	Lik	Likiang	Na	Nanshah	Ra	Rameswaram	Tu	Tulaimannar
Ka	Kalewa	M	Manipur	P	Pienmu	S	Sumprabum	W	Wangting
Ke	Keng Tung	Mahm	Mahmoudabad	Pa	Paoshan	Sar	Sarikamish	Wh	Wenshen
Ku	Kukieng	Mg	Mongwa	Po	Poseh	SG	Saikhan Ghat	Y	Yungning

te: Boundaries between North Yunnan and North Burma, and Tibet and China are according to Chinese documents

EUROPE AND THE FAR EAST

Before the war, you could fly from London to Hongkong in about one week, or go by water in about three weeks, or take the train to Vladivostok in ten days. This last is the only really modern "ground" communication between Europe and the Far East. There is, however, an alternate. Take the train to Sergiopol on the Turk-Sib Railway—if you can persuade the Russians to let you!—and there, if you cannot fly from Hami, change to one of two means of transportation, motor truck or camel. If you get a truck and it does not break down during the 1770-mile trek, you can hope to reach Lanchow in about fifteen days; a camel does not break down, but if you rely on him the same little trip to Lanchow might take 120 days. (From Lanchow to Chungking is 1300 miles farther.) This is pretty fast going, particularly if you remember it took Marco Polo and his father and his uncle very much longer to reach Peiping from Venice. (But, on the other hand, it should be said, at the height of Mongol power, the pony-express system of the Great Khans made the trip from Kiev to China in the incredible time of 168 days.)

From all of which it ought to be clear that any large body of men wishing, during the present war, to go from the two major oceans across Asia, had better take the Trans-Siberian Railway, and remember, if the color of their passports or the strength of their arms permit, to take the short cut across Manchuria formerly called the Chinese Eastern, rather than the longer way around Manchuria on Russian soil.

This is a good solid railway, lately double-tracked. Americans wishing to reach Russia with a minimum of sea-sickness will probably get to Komsomolsk in Siberia as best they can (and via the Alaska Highway this should not be too difficult) and thence to China and Russia.

Equally interesting—strategically—is the line from Komsomolsk southward to Voroshilov near Vladivostok, thence westward to Harbin, and south into China right to Hankow on the Yangtse River, which is joined by a railroad from Korea and Japan. There is no bridge over the vast Yangtse, but you can cross on a ferryboat to Wu-chang on the south bank, get into another train and continue south to Hengyang, where the rail from Shanghai comes in. Change here for a train to Liuchow. Here you have to get out and take to the open as far as Chennankwan on the Indo Chinese frontier, either "afoot and light hearted," or in a military truck, depending on whether you are a poet or a Japanese soldier. At Chennankwan you can pile into another train that will take you far south, right through Indo China to Saigon. From Saigon, a railroad track runs all the way to Singapore by way of Bangkok in Thailand.

This means that the immense strategic zone stretching from Kamchatka to Singapore has its main sea connections paralleled by an almost complete railroad. Once these two routes come into the hands of a single power, then any operations against that power almost necessarily become amphibian and possibly aerial as well. Or, concretely expressed, to drive the Japs out of their *blitz* conquests requires not only to defeat them at sea but very likely to make numerous landings on the continent of Asia as well. Unless it can be done by simultaneous sea and air attack at the heart of Nippon itself. Or unless Chinese and Russians striking from inland can do the land portion of the operations.

This last is not particularly difficult. For in a struggle between Russia and Japan,

See also pages 15, 51, 105.

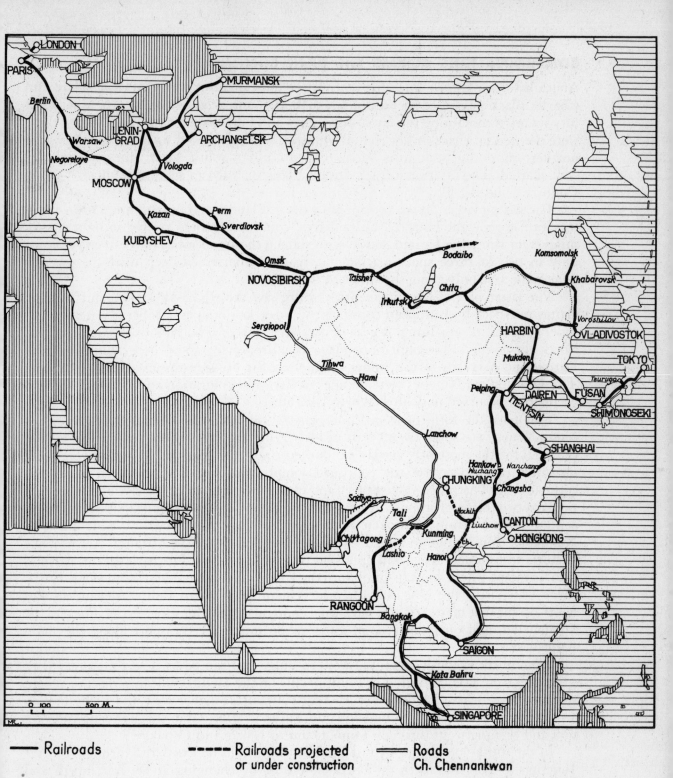

Russian troops have the same advantage over Japan as German troops in Europe over British—they are continentally based and supplied and have plenty of territory to retire into; they can strike at the heart of their enemy while the Japanese can at best do no more than wound one of Russia's outstretched arms.

COMMUNICATIONS ACROSS THE DARK CONTINENT

Africa has been known since the dawn of civilization. But when in 1867 Adam and Charles Black published in Edinburgh their *General Atlas of the World,* "a series of fifty-six maps containing the latest discoveries and new boundaries," just four of these were devoted to Africa. A few coastal countries were portrayed with fair accuracy—the northern shore, Egypt and the Sudan (called Nubia), South Africa; the coastline was well charted. The interior was left largely blank or filled in by inscriptions, "Gorilla Country," and the like.

The second largest of the continents, a mass of land five thousand miles from north to south, forty-eight hundred miles across, comprising some twelve million square miles (four times the United States) with sixteen thousand miles of coasts, was known only in two or three spots. Lacking navigable estuaries or deep inlets, it was impenetrable save only along the valley of the Nile.

The latter part of the nineteenth century saw the wholesale staking-out of huge claims in Africa by European countries; in 1935 Ethiopia and Liberia were the last independent bits remaining. A year or two later, Ethiopia had disappeared and Africa stood out as merely a giant appendage of Europe, separated geographically from Europe and Asia only by the "inner channel" of the Mediterranean with the Red Sea. The Eighties and Nineties were decades of African exploration and nominal seizure: occupation occurred only after World War One.

This took the form of a multiple penetration from the circumference into the center. There are some twenty rail heads serving thirty or more coastal towns, but the lines for the most part simply run a piece into the interior and stop. Even today no single railroad crosses the continent longitudinally, nor is any such in serious construction. The much talked of "Cape to Cairo" railroad is yet to come, although perhaps two-thirds of it exist in broken bits. From Capetown or Port Elizabeth you can go north by train to Broken Hill. There a road brings you in a wide curve to Niamkolo. You change to a boat. At Kigoma by rail again to Mwanza. Across Lake Victoria to Entebbe. Then rail and road to Juba when you hit the Nile and descend it to Taragma where you can climb into the Khartoum train and go on to Wadi Halfa. More water, still the Nile, and then at Assuan by train to Cairo, Alexandria and Suez—or, for that matter, if you have time enough, across Palestine, Syria, Turkey, the Dardanelles, and on to Narvik in Norway. So much for transport along the main African axis.

From north to south across the western bulge you can go by desert motorcar with supertires from French Algiers or Philippeville on the Mediterranean across the Sahara straight on to British Lagos or French Port Harcourt. Further west, the Vichy French are hurriedly finishing the Trans-Saharan Railroad from Oran through Gao to Cotonou and turning west, through Timbouctou to Dakar and Conakry.

In the south you can go by rail from Swakopmund or Luederitz through De Aar Junction to Port Elizabeth or East London, or by changing at De Aar, north and, east, to Durban, Lourenço Marques or Beira. Better, you may travel behind a locomotive from Lobito on the Atlantic Coast by Tenge to Broken Hill, then to Beira or to Dar-es-Salaam on the Indian Ocean. In all this is much confusion and delay. A useful transversal overland route is from Douala by rail to Yaoundé, from there by

See also page 97.

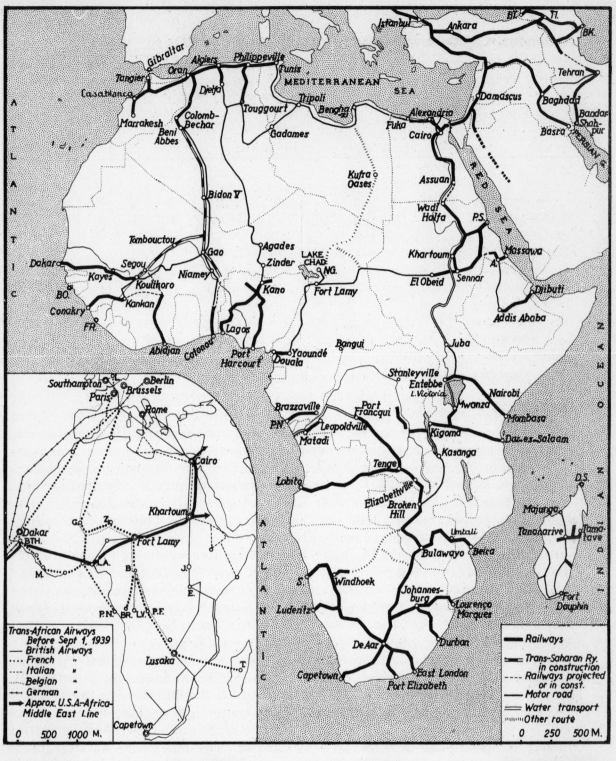

Trans-African Airways
Before Sept 1, 1939
——— British Airways "
········· French "
·─·─·─ Italian "
- - - - Belgian "
+++++ German "
——➤ Approx. U.S.A-Africa-
Middle East Line

0   500   1000 M.

——— Railways
══ Trans-Saharan Ry.
     in construction
- - - - Railways projected
     or in const.
——— Motor road
═══ Water transport
········· Other route

0   250   500 M.

A	Asmara	BTH	Bathurst
B	Bangui	DS	Diego Suarez
BK	Baku	E	Entebbe
BO	Bolama	FR	Freetown
BR	Brazzaville	G	Gao
BT	Batum	J	Juba

L	London	PN	Pointe Noire
La	Lagos	PS	Port Sudan
LV	Leopoldville	S	Swakopmund
M	Monrovia	T	Tananarive
NG	Ngouri	TI	Tiflis
PF	Port Francqui	Z	Zinder

truck north to Port Lamy on the southern edge of the Great Desert and thence on east to the railhead at El Obeid in the Sudan. My sister-in-law and another woman did this easily in a truck they drove themselves.

But by far the finest route hardly touches the ground at all. American semi-official commercial planes bring you from the Atlantic coast of the United States to Lagos. Thence another plane will take you to the Sudan and still another carry you high over the Nile to Cairo. Many other such airlines were in operation before the war, Belgian, French, British, notably the Cape to Cairo route, opened in 1931. New ones are planned by Vichy Frenchmen.

In the last analysis it will be neither rail nor road but the airpaths that will bring modern man into Africa and thereby Africa into civilization. Meanwhile the truck haul across Africa's waist and the airline above it are revolutionizing Near Eastern strategy and can substitute in part for a closed Mediterranean.

The opening of the new French railroad in West Central Africa will bring the West African Coast in close touch with Morocco, Algeria, Spain and France. If this means anything, it is that the holder of North Africa has a terrific head start in the race to dominate the West African ports. These ports are the natural springboards for a leap into South America, and enable their holders to bring ships through coastal waters all the way from Europe.

In these facts there is dynamite

AUSTRALIA

This is the smallest of the continents and the largest of the islands. It comprises no less than one-fifth of the entire British Commonwealth of Nations. It is as large as the United States. And it is inhabited by no more than seven million people. These people are enterprising and fearless; they are easy going; they fight well. But they have not been able really to settle their homeland or properly to develop it. If their island had not lain completely off the world routes (though a sort of corner pillar to the Indian Ocean), it would have been fiercely contested long before this. Geologically it is part of Oceania (the Pacific Mediterranean). Raising the sea bottom around the island by but two hundred feet would join it to New Guinea and to Tasmania.

Australia is conveniently divided into three portions, the Western Plateau, comprising most of the west and torrid north; the Central Lowlands stretching across vast areas and in part arid, and the Southeastern Highlands. Here on one-sixth of the land, almost all the people and the industry are concentrated.

Since a large portion of the land is barren unless intensely irrigated, the seven million people thought they had better to do than develop it. Since most of the places they wished to go could be reached only by ship, rail development was backward—and incredible. Australians deny this: they insist that per head their country has more miles of railroad than any other country—which is quite exact. They omit currently to add that per square mile—as the accompanying map amply demonstrates—there is less railroad than anywhere else but in Brazil and Egypt. If existing lines were all of one gauge, it might not be so bad. They are not. As the map shows, they comprise three systems, broad gauge, standard gauge and narrow gauge. You can go from Sydney to Albury and from Augusta to Kalgoorlie on standard rails but you cannot go from Sydney to Melbourne (the two chief cities) without changing trains. And

See also page 55.

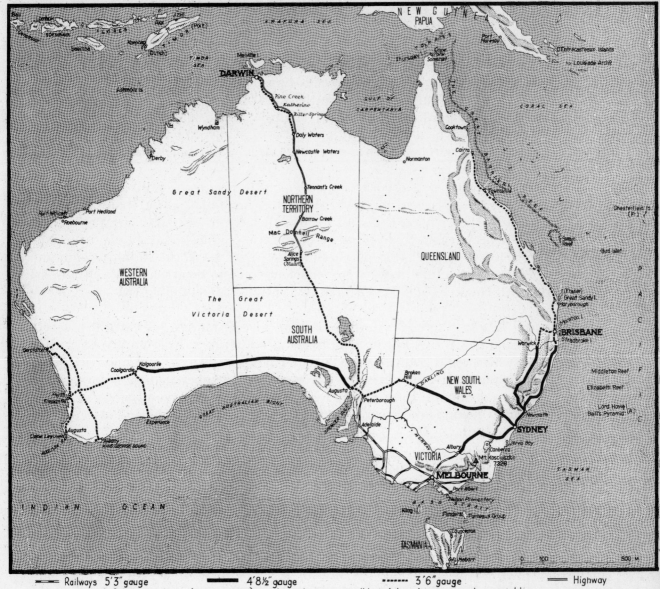

Railways 5'3" gauge — 4'8½" gauge ------- 3'6" gauge === Highway

Only main railways (transcontinental) are shown, the termini of all branch lines leading from the coastal lines to the interior are marked on the map by points.

there is no through line from the south to the north of the country. The middle stage across the MacDonnell Range is made by road.

The island gives a good living to seven millions but is only fairly well endowed with natural resources. It exports wheat and wool; there is coal and a fair amount of iron, as well as other metals. Most of the mining interests are in the south. Industries were rapidly developed only during this war.

For all these reasons Australia is extremely hard to defend. Save by air, its defenders, necessarily limited in numbers, can hardly be quickly concentrated at any point likely to be attacked.

But for the same reasons it is extremely difficult to invade and almost impossible to conquer. It is a fair though by no means a sure bet that Axis aggressors, rather than try to seize and occupy this vast, flat empty continent, will try to go round, isolate its defenders and neutralize them.

COMMUNICATIONS ACROSS NORTH AND CENTRAL AMERICA

Of all the large land masses, North America has the best lateral communications. Two almost completely separated railroads cross Canada from Halifax to Prince Rupert and Vancouver, with a single strategic bottleneck at Winnepeg. At Dawson Creek, the Canadian National joins the new Alaska Highway which may, in a not too distant future, be paralleled by a railroad from Seattle to Nome. For it must never be forgotten that no motor transport has ever succeeded in rivalling a railroad as a mass carrier of people or things.

The United States is completely crossed by at least four trunk railroads and though Chicago knots most of them together, alternate routes through St. Louis and New Orleans have large carrying capacity. Even with Detroit and New Orleans both in enemy hands, heavy traffic could be maintained between the two oceans via the middle routes. Reinforced by the finest system of highways in the world, military communications across the United States seem sufficient for any emergency. The transport system of this country could stand more concentrated air bombing than any other— and still carry on.

Central America, though relatively lacking in communications, is still theoretically well supplied with transversal railroads. Vera Cruz to Manzanillo, Vera Cruz and Puerto Mexico to Salina Cruz, Puerto Barrios to San Jose; Limon to Punta Arenas; Cristobal to Balboa. But it is necessary to remember that these lines are in extremely bad condition. Even if they were not, they could serve invaders as well as defenders and under some circumstances, Americans might come to curse the day they had been built.

Longitudinally, American communications are less satisfactory. The projected Pan-American highway is still "spotty" and there is no great thoroughfare from Maine or Seattle to Panama. North-south railroads are rare in the Pacific Northwest. Northern Mexico, however, has three converging on Mexico City. From there down a single line goes as far south as Fonseca Bay, but it is slow and disjointed.

On the whole, however, communications on the North American Continent are admirable. Even without counting their possession of the largest existing fleet of transport planes, the North Americans, if they stand together, have all possible facilities for the most rapid large-scale concentration of men and material ever made. After the Pearl Harbor disaster, Secretary of War Stimson had no difficulty in transporting several hundred thousand troops over long distances with no disturbance of normal communication. This applies to transshipments as well. In wartime, when expense is of no consequence, when ships are more exposed to attack than coasts, transport of supplies across North America is easier and quicker (even including time lost in loading and reloading at the coasts) than sending them by sea through the Panama Canal.

See also pages 111 to 117.

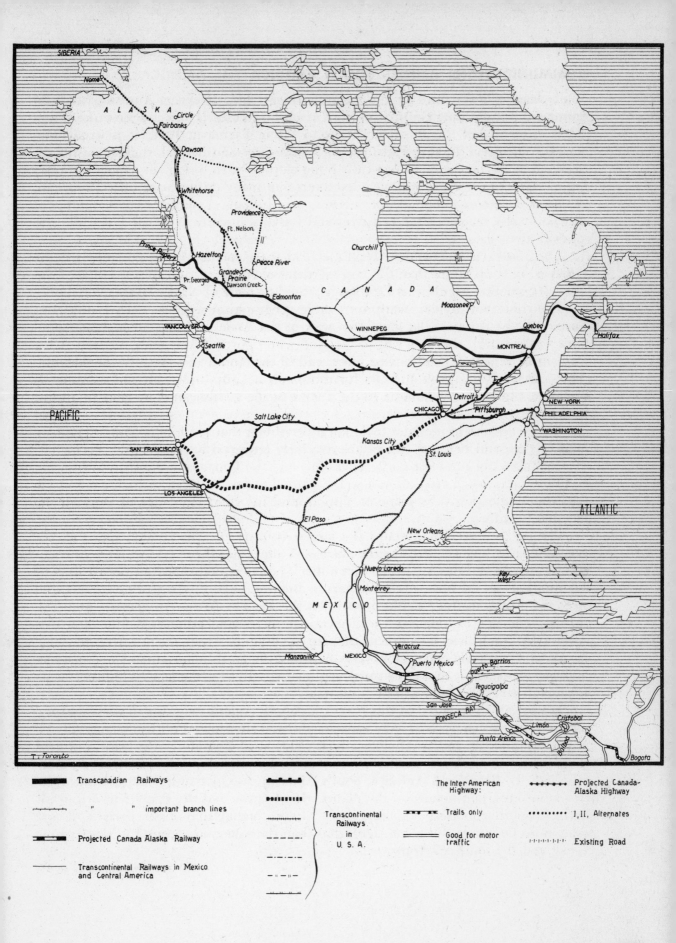

SIBERIA

Nome

A L A S K A   Circle
Fairbanks

Dawson

Whitehorse

Providence
Ft. Nelson   II
Prince Rupert   Hazelton   Peace River
Pr. Georges   Grande   Churchill
                Prairie
              Dawson Creek   C A N A D A
                Edmonton   Moosonee

VANCOUVER   WINNIPEG   Quebec
        Seattle   Halifax
                                              MONTREAL

PACIFIC   Detroit   NEW YORK
                              Salt Lake City   CHICAGO   Pittsburgh   PHILADELPHIA
                                                               WASHINGTON
SAN FRANCISCO   Kansas City
                                        St. Louis
LOS ANGELES
                                                                    ATLANTIC
                    El Paso
                              New Orleans
                                                    Key
                                                    West
                    Nuevo Laredo
                      Monterrey
              M E X I C O
Manzanillo   MEXICO   Veracruz
                        Puerto Mexico   Puerto Barrios
                                    Tegucigalpa
          Salina Cruz   San José
                        FONSECA BAY   Cristobal
                              Punta Arenas   Limón
                                        Balboa   Bogota

T: Toronto

▬▬▬▬ Transcanadian Railways	▬▬▬▬	The Inter American Highway:	•••••• Projected Canada-Alaska Highway
―――― " " important branch lines	■■■■■■■	▬▬▬ Trails only	•••••••• I, II, Alternates
▬▭▬ Projected Canada Alaska Railway	Transcontinental Railways in U.S.A.	═══ Good for motor traffic	ιιιιιιιι Existing Road
―――― Transcontinental Railways in Mexico and Central America	――――		
	― ― ―		
	― · · ―		
	― " ― "		
	ιιιιιιιιι		

75

COMMUNICATIONS ACROSS SOUTH AMERICA

South America is the third largest of the continents and, excepting Australia, the least populated. From Punta Gallinas in the Caribbean to Cape Horn is 4700 miles. From Natal at the tip of the Brazilian Bulge to Punta Parina in Peru, it is 3150 miles across. It hangs on the thin Panamanian Isthmus like an inverted, slightly misshapen pear and seems, on the usual vertically hung map, to be in imminent danger of breaking off. Of its ninety-one million inhabitants, not many millions are pure European; the rest are mestizos of one sort or another, pure Indians or pure Negro. A number of still politically unassimilated Germans and Italians, notably in Brazil and Chile, are an explosive element.

There are ten independent republics and three smaller European colonies, the Guianas. Brazil is larger than the United States of America—and largely empty. Uruguay, the smallest republic, is little larger than the State of North Dakota.

The continent divides neatly into three geographical sections, each facing on a separate body of water: the long strip west of the Andes, the second highest mountains in the world; the strip east of the Andes and north of the giant Amazon River Valley; the remaining and largest piece, east of the Andes and south of the Amazon. The Amazon is navigable literally for thousands of miles upstream and its valley is immense, but from the Amazon to the Pacific or the Caribbean is by land an all but impossible trek.

The western strip includes the 2600 mile ribbon that is Chile, a little of Bolivia, most of Peru and Ecuador. There are relatively few good harbors on the Pacific.

Colombia (for the most part), Venezuela and the Guianas face northward on the Caribbean and are of vital interest to the United States. Between this section and the rest, communication is by plane or ship around the Brazilian bulge or through the Panama Canal.

The Atlantic section contains the largest country, Brazil, divided into two not very well co-ordinated pieces by the Amazon Valley; and the two most modern countries, Uruguay and the Argentine Republic. The only good transcontinental lines of communication, the railroads, both start at Buenos Aires, the Argentine capital, and cross the Andes to three Chilean ports on the Pacific: Arica, Antofagasta and Valparaiso. The line to Valparaiso was never completed and a hundred mile stretch is covered by motor, which lengthens the trip to 36 hours. From Buenos Aires to Antofagasta and Arica takes about four days. Much of the great longitudinal Pan-American highway exists and it should be completed in 1943. But for the lack of improvements it remains what the army calls a "task road."

Strategically, the moral of this is simple: South America consists of three isolated sections comprising 13 relatively isolated political divisions. Political cooperation is physically difficult and psychologically problematic. Therefore, the vast continent constitutes one of the most effective strategical barriers that exist, comparable only to Africa. Unlike North America, South America does not unite, but separates the two most important oceans on the planet, the Atlantic and the Pacific, by a difficult barrier. South American strategy seems almost bound to remain peripheral and economic. The continent is less significant than the waterways around it, the Panama Canal and the southern straits.

See also pages 37 to 45.

C   Cordoba
CU Curityba
J   Jujuy
R   Rosario
TR Treinta y Tres

C   to Colombia
EC to Ecuador
Ch to Chile

III. NATURAL ROUTES OF INVASION

THE NORTH EUROPEAN PLAIN

This has been one of the most inviting battlefields of the globe. From Leningrad to Le Havre, pleasant, flat rich country borders the Baltic and North Sea. Most of Russia is less than six hundred feet above salt water. As you go westward, this zone narrows and reaches its narrowest in Belgium. Even here you have a couple of hundred miles along the water before you reach the steep wooded hills of the Ardennes. But why limit yourself to the coastal plain when, except for the few areas shown on the map, almost none of this area is higher than fifteen hundred feet?

The rivers from the Dvina (Riga) to the Seine run in a northern or northwesterly direction—friendly European rivers neither too wide nor too swift to be crossed at will and provide routes rather than obstacles. The terrain is so flat that it has been possible to join them up in one vast river-canal system from the English Channel all the way to the Dnieper and the remote Black Sea. In short, here is a piece of land offering unlimited movement to the many peoples who have crossed and recrossed it.

Present ease of communications is demonstrated by the distribution of population. Here again the zones run in an east-westerly direction. Along the Baltic Coast there is a relatively thinly inhabited strip (under 125 persons to the square mile). As you go south, the density increases: a second zone stretches right across the continent from Soviet Russia to the Zuyder Zee. Within it, a narrower ribbon of dense population (250 to 500 per square mile) winds its way from Eastern Europe to the Straits of Dover. Coal deposits and great trading or manufacturing centers have attracted islands of even thicker populations.

The North European Plain holds historical battlefields galore. Here Swedes, Germans, Austrians, French engaged in the ruinous free-for-all that was called the Thirty Years' War. Here Prussians wrested provinces from Austrians and lost the Palatinate and Alsace to Frenchmen. Three times in the memory of the living, Germans have joined issue with Frenchmen on these plains. In the Low Countries, Englishmen, Dutch, Flemings, Walloons, Burgundians, Luxembourgers, Spaniards, French, Germans and Austrians have slugged out their quarrels. Nowhere more than in Belgium has history been made.

It is still the same—but with an important difference: the Northern European Plain has become too small for the available armies. Even in World War One the terrain from the Alps to the North Sea offered no room for maneuver. Soldiers packed into trenches like sardines in cans, fought in "continuous lines" right across the map until the least numerous side collapsed from exhaustion. In World War Two, the Germans took Poland with sixty or seventy divisions and the Netherlands, Belgium and France with not more than twice this number—a little more than half the forces theoretically available. Where would they have found room for their flocks of bombing planes and their herds of tanks?

For war to regain its ancient status as an art, with the fullest employment of modern weapons, vaster fields were necessary—the gigantic plain that is Russia, the limitless African sands, the Middle Eastern semi-wastes from the Mediterranean and the Black Sea to the Persian Gulf, the plateau of Central Asia, Lowland China—or the Mississippi Valley! Modern war has outgrown the North European Plain and areas where once decisive battles made history can now house mere episodes of Global Struggle.

See also page 21.

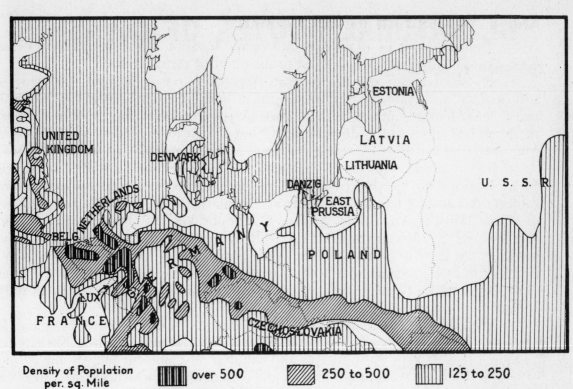

Density of Population per. sq. Mile
||| over 500   **////** 250 to 500   **||||** 125 to 250

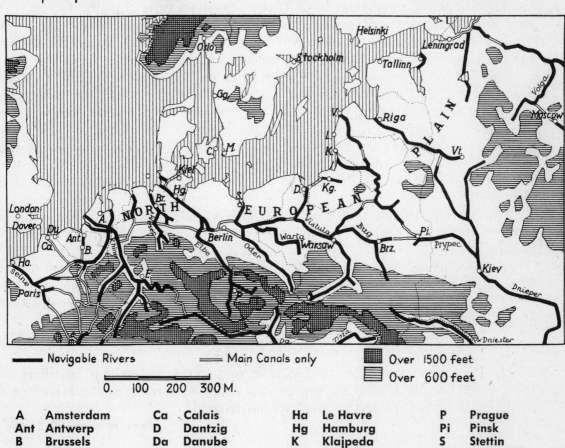

—— Navigable Rivers   ══ Main Canals only   ▓ Over 1500 feet   ▒ Over 600 feet

0.   100   200   300 M.

A	Amsterdam	**Ca**	Calais	**Ha**	Le Havre	**P**	Prague
Ant	Antwerp	**D**	Dantzig	**Hg**	Hamburg	**Pi**	Pinsk
B	Brussels	**Da**	Danube	**K**	Klajpeda	**S**	Stettin
Br	Bremen	**Du**	Dunkirk	**Kg**	Koenigsberg	**V**	Ventspils
Brz	Brzesc	**F**	Frankfurt	**L**	Liepaja	**Vi**	Vitebsk
C	Copenhagen	**Gg**	Göteburg	**M**	Malmö		

AND IF YOU SHOULD INVADE GERMANY

It is a Prussian habit to attack first and escape invasion. Nazi Germany was essentially Prussia, enlarged and worsened to the point of caricature.

When Adolf Hitler and the German Army took power in 1933, Germany was still the most vulnerable of countries, open to invasion from France, Czechoslovakia and Poland. By the summer of 1942, after six years of secret and three of open war, the Nazis had succeeded in dominating all but the Russian portion of the European Continent and had bitten into that as far as a line from Lake Ladoga to the Sea of Azov. Italy, Finland, Hungary, Roumania and Bulgaria were satelite confederates. Vichy France with North Africa and Franco Spain were neutral puppets actually subject to German orders. Poland, Norway, Denmark, the Netherlands, Belgium, most of France, Albania, Yugoslavia, Austria, Czechoslovakia and Greece were conquered and occupied. Sweden and Switzerland, while truly neutral, worked for the Nazi war machine. On the European Continent only Portugal and Turkey enjoyed a sort of problematic independence. All in all, a tremendous achievement, despite the failure of the air assault on Great Britain and of the tank offensives against Egypt from Italian Libya.

By all this the Axis accomplished several things. It avoided a two-front war and rendered communications between the Soviets and the other United Nations long and circuitous. It kept the initiative and could at any moment launch one or more of several offensives from inside lines, while considerable United Nations forces were immobilized outside awaiting Adolf Hitler's good pleasure. Finally, Germany, the soul of the Axis, was well cushioned by distance against actual attack. As a result, Germany and Italy might, subject only to wholesale bombing, go on the defensive and challenge the United Nations to come and dig them out.

There were however some flaws in this situation. The Italians had shown so little stomach for a Nazi war that much of Italy had to be garrisoned like a conquered country. The beaten peoples were restive and it took considerable Axis forces and ceaseless executions to keep them down. French Africa, though purged of many elements by the Vichy regime, might still welcome United Nations invasion. So might the majority of Spaniards. The Nazis had extended themselves along the 2000-3000 miles of coastline from the Pyrenees to the Arctic Ocean, and simply could not garrison it all.

Theoretically, therefore, so long as the Soviets could continue to engage the bulk of the Germans, the United Nations forces could, once they were ready, choose several sorts of attack.

(1) They could, from bases in Iceland and Britain, try to join forces with the Russians in Northern Norway, thereby securing their communications.

(2) They could from Narvik move southward across Norway and try to establish air bases at Stavanger and Oslo.

(3) They could land directly opposite the British Isles and seek to establish permanent bridgeheads.

(4) They could make Commando raids or permanent landings anywhere from Brest south, notably around St. Nazaire, and count on a rising of the French people to aid them in establishing a broad second front.

See also pages 15, 21 and 61.

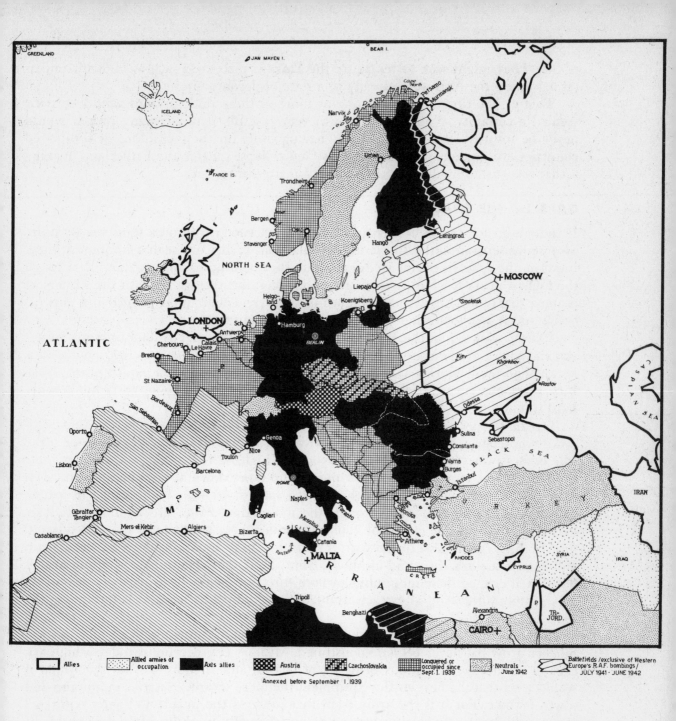

Allies | Allied armies of occupation | Axis allies | Austria | Czechoslovakia | Conquered or occupied since Sept. 1, 1939 | Neutrals – June 1942 | Battlefields /exclusive of Western Europe's R.A.F. bombings/ JULY 1941 - JUNE 1942

Annexed before September 1, 1939

(5) They could land in Portugal or Spain and compel the Germans to divert heavy forces to keep them at bay.

(6) They might—with or without the assistance of the Free French—land and take over French West and North Africa and once established, use this as a base for the invasion of Italy, on the vulnerable "soft" side of the Axis.

(7) They might attempt the same from Libya, having prepared an Italian uprising against the Germans by an appropriate intellectual and psychological offensive.

(8) They might seek to recapture the Balkans piecemeal—a most difficult undertaking unless the Axis were already in a state of decomposition.

That at one time or another one or more of these undertakings would be tried seemed a certainty. Nonetheless, it was very possible that Germany proper would never be invaded—that the Germans, having built up their cushions of conquered countries, would defend them to the last and collapse *outside* the Fatherland, making actual occupation by the United Nations a matter of routine.

GAPS IN THE PYRENEES

If there are such things as "natural frontiers" between countries then the Pyrenees Mountains separating the Iberian Peninsula from France are such a frontier. Stretching from the Atlantic to the Mediterranean, they definitely constitute a wall. Though the highest peaks reach only to about 11,000 feet, the average height of the Pyrenees is above that of the Alps. And on the whole the Pyrenees are more rugged and impenetrable—more like that other mountain wall, the Caucasus.

"Never walk far in the Pyrenees without two days' reserve food on your back," was the advice of one trained mountaineer who knows these stern craggy mountains better than most. Storms are frequent with sudden drops of temperature (one June First I was once turned back by a blinding snowstorm at about 6000 feet). Shelters are hard to find.

On the steeper French side, there are great natural amphitheaters, the "cirques," down whose steep sides unnumbered streams come tumbling with clouds of spray (the highest waterfall at Gavarnie is 1500 feet high).

The Pyrenees are highest in the middle and taper down at both ends. Along each coast runs a railroad, broken at the Franco-Spanish frontier by a change in gauge; two more small lines dodge through the mountains. Passes are high, few and far between. In this whole extent of about 300 miles there are but five motor roads and four of them closed most of the year. Truly, the land communications between Spain and France are not easy, and although from the days of Hannibal, invading armies have often crossed these mountains in both directions, each invasion was a feat of no mean importance. And after each, the frontier established itself as before along the Pyrenees watershed.

Just how much of an obstacle these mountains would constitute to a well-equipped modern army has never been demonstrated. Military engineering is today a high art, capable of almost miraculous bridging of chasms and streams. Yet on the whole it would seem that the heavier the equipment the more serious obstacles mountains and towns become. For it is the army train that presents the problem—lightly equipped mountain infantry can go anywhere and climb virtually anything, often dragging light artillery with them into positions once considered inaccessible. Positions on high crags are supplied by cable railways with hanging cars. But tanks, even light tanks, cannot go bounding across mountainsides and where roads can be blasted into precipices, heavy equipment just has to halt. For this reason, all rough high mountains and the Pyrenees in particular would seem to confer a signal advantage upon defenders.

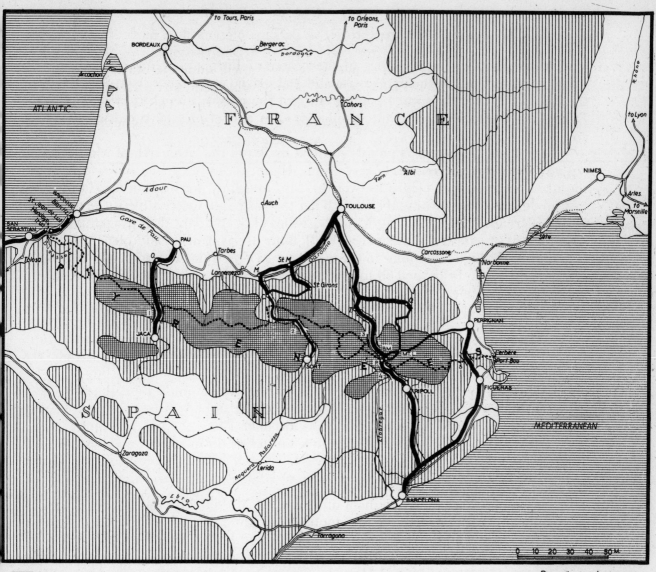

Mountains approx. above 5000 feet	Main highways	Main railways	Boundaries between France, Spain, Andorra
Mountains approx. above 2000 feet	secondary highways	Railways crossing the Pyrenees	canals

1 Somport 4343′
2 Port de la Bonaigua 6216′
3 Col de Puymorens 5745′
4 Tosas Pass 5400′

5 Le Perthus 880′
C Cierp
BM Bourg Madame
M Montrejean

MtL Mont Louis
StM Saint Martory
O Oloron Sainte Marie
Q Quillan

P Puigcerda
T Tarascon

THE ALPINE PASSES

The lumpy mass of the Alps lies in the center of Europe and divides Italy from France, Switzerland, Germany, Austria and Jugoslavia, and France from Austria and the Balkans. Hence the supreme importance of the routes through these mountains. From time immemorial migrant peoples, traders and armies have crossed and re-crossed the high passes.

Mont Blanc, the highest summit—dubbed by Byron the "Monarch of Mountains" —is an exhausting but relatively easy climb. Hannibal got credit he did not deserve for taking an army with elephants over the Alps into Italy, for his brother Hasdrubal had no difficulty in repeating the trick. That the passes are inaccessible is the sheerest legend. Perhaps it has grown up with the stories of St. Bernard dogs dragging frozen travelers out of monstrous avalanches. Well, there are avalanches and plenty of snow. But actually no high mountains in the world are so accessible, with so many relatively low passes that can be crossed on foot or on skis all year round in good weather, without excessive trouble.

Here is a list of the chief ones, two of which are not shown on the map:

	feet above sea level		feet above sea level
Mont Genèvre Pass	6102	St. Gotthard	6935
Mont Cenis	6834	Maloja Pass	5942
Little St. Bernard	7179	Bernina Pass	7645
Col de la Seigne	8242	Brenner Pass	4495
Big St. Bernard	8111	Loibl Pass	4881
Simplon Pass	6592		

That no one cared to live in them until the late Middle Ages was largely a matter of emotional distaste. People thought mountains ugly. Even poets cursed the "scowling barren crags" and hurried down into the smiling Italian plains or onward to the cheery tavern firesides of Basel or Innsbruck. Perhaps it was dislike of mountains that brought one Swiss family called Habsburg from the north Alpine slopes to the Emperor's palace at Schoenbrunn near Vienna. Only in the last century, under the impetus of the romantic authors, winter sports and hygiene, could a tiny Confederation of villagers develop into a fine rich country through an unrivaled combination of military valor, untiring industry and salesmanship.

Where travelers could come and go, armies found crossing relatively easy. Barbarians from Germany got down to Rome, Roman armies marched out to take Gaul and Switzerland and the Danube Valley—all without much trouble. The old Romans, like Hannibal, preferred the Mont Genèvre Pass and the Brenner. The Mont Cenis is first mentioned in the year 756 A.D. A Russian Army under Suvarof made a legendary passage across Switzerland in the time of Napoleon.

It was the railroads that first made the Alps a military barrier. For railroads meant tunnels—at least ten of them important. Tunnels went under mountains and could be dynamited. Caved-in tunnels promised traffic obstruction, not for weeks but for years. Therefore, putative invaders pause before the hardy mountaineer with the

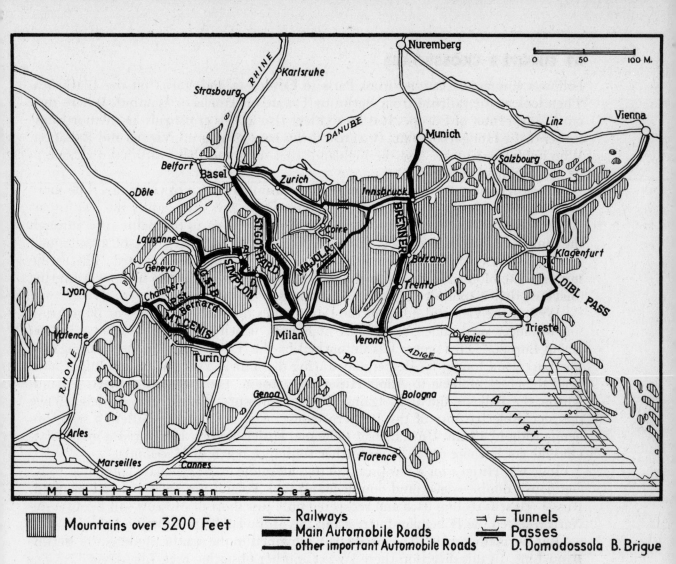

Mountains over 3200 Feet | Railways | Tunnels
Main Automobile Roads | Passes
other important Automobile Roads | D. Domodossola B. Brigue

TNT in his hand. Moreover, the more warfare becomes technical, the more rough ground becomes a barrier—not the less. Alpine roads can really be made impassable for tanks and Alpine rock shelters can defy the most terrific bombings.

At least five highly important main routes out of Italy traverse the Alps. Another bores through them from west to east from Basel to Innsbruck. It might well develop that the guardians of the high passes have acquired a new military importance unsuspected by former ages.

AT EUROPE'S CROSSROADS

Follow a line across Europe from Paris to Constanta and Varna on the Black Sea. Then look at the railroad from Berlin to Trieste or Athens or Istanbul. Where they cross is the center of Europe. It is no accident that at this crossroads, in the northwest corner of the Hungarian plain, two great towns have sprung up, Vienna and Budapest. Who holds these towns, and the highlands that surround them, still has a chance to be the master of Europe.

From here not one but two main roads lead northward into Germany. The more westerly, through Prague into Saxony, is historically and strategically the less important of the two. To the east, the venerable "Amber Road" to the Baltic runs through the famous *Moravian Gap,* the only real break in the northern line of mountains— Erz, Sudetens, Carpathians—that form the Central European watershed. This is the storied route of "barbarian" invasion of the Danube Valley. It was here, at Austerlitz (Slavkov) that Napoleon smashed the Russians.

West of the Gap and north of the Danube lies the natural fortress of Bohemia, a sort of saucer surrounded by wooded highlands, which Bismarck declared was "the key to Europe." This saucer was untouched by the Tartar invasion, held out against the Turks, was fought for desperately during the Thirty Years' War, and might have been the chief obstacle to Adolf Hitler's expansion. For Bohemia protects Poland, Russia, the Balkans and Italy against German pressure—and Austria as well. Hence the incredible frivolity of the Western democracies in allowing Hitler to seize Bohemia without a fight. Until he had Bohemia, Hitler did not dare to risk a major war. Once he got it, there could be no further resistance north of Macedonia.

Italy was Hitler's for a few promises to a megalomaniac. Hungary consented to be Germany's double-edged (and double-faced) tool. Poland was encircled and smashed. Russia was sent reeling back and recovered only just short of Moscow—all because the Nazis received the Bohemian fortress and the Moravian Gap without a fight.

But Germany's main drive necessarily remained to the southeast along the Berlin-Basra Line. In this direction there lay yet another obstacle—Free Jugoslavia.

Follow the Danube downstream from Budapest and you come to Belgrade crouching on its bluff above two rivers. A little further east comes in the Morava (not to be confused with the Moravian Gap). Here railroad and highway turn south and begin to ascend. This is the Serbian river *par excellence* and takes you through the heart of the country. At Nis you can turn eastward again and cross difficult country to Bulgarian Sofia and Turkish Istanbul. But the shortest road to blue water continues south and climbs higher and higher until you enter Macedonia and reach the headwaters near Skoplje (called Uskub by the Turks).

The Skoplje Pass is one of the strongest defensive situations in the world and a better-prepared Serbian army might have held it. Once over the pass, you (and the train you are on) descend through the storied Vardar Valley that beckons you down to Salonika and Greece.

Yet militarily it is not enough to possess the Skoplje Pass. A successful *Drang* demands that the Morava and Vardar Valleys be kept permanently open for absolutely vital communications. They can easily be raided from the mountains to the west. These Balkan mountains are wild country, dangerous to any invader. Here centuries

ago Serbian peasants made their last desperate stand against the Turks at Kossovo. And here in World War Two, Major Draja Mihailovitch rallied the beaten Serbs and challenged German communications.

Twice in a century Germans bent on plunder have had to conquer Serbia in order to pursue their *Drang nach Osten*.

At the end of World War One, Germany's downfall began with defeat in the Vardar Valley....

THE BALTIC SEA

The Baltic Sea and the Black Sea are the gills of Soviet Russia—and so undersized that the Russians continually gasp for salt water.

The Baltic Sea is a long, relatively narrow, irregularly shaped, pale blue, shallow body of water separating the Scandinavian Peninsula from the European Continent. It covers about 160,000 square miles. At the upper end it forks into three gulfs: the long, deep, cold Gulf of Bothnia between Sweden and Finland; the much smaller Gulf of Finland between Finland and Esthonia with Soviet Russia at the end; and the pouch-like Gulf of Riga between Esthonia and Latvia. At the bottom it turns and leads northward through three channels: the Big Belt; the Little Belt; and the Sund—into the Kattegat, which in turn becomes the Skagerrak and the North Sea.

At one geological period it was connected with the Arctic Ocean through what is now northern Finland. At another it was entirely a fresh-water lake. Even now, because of the 250 streams that enter into it, its waters are only slightly saline and its surface is several inches above ocean level. Tides are negligible and navigation is easy save for shoals, sudden storms and winter ice. (In the old days it allegedly froze clear across on occasion; even now the Gulf of Finland at Leningrad is often ice-covered for 150 days of the year, though navigation can proceed behind ice-breakers.)

By cutting the Kiel Canal from Holtenau near Kiel to Brunsbuettel near the mouth of the Elbe, the Germans reduced the distance to the sea by about five hundred miles. Sixty-one miles of sea-level canal allowed their fleet to choose between the Baltic and North Sea. Incidentally, this canal is an important world highway that has seen the passage of as much as seven million tons of freight annually.

The effect of the Baltic has been to make the climate of the surrounding countries distinctly milder than say, Soviet Russia or Canada in similar latitudes.

Several sorts of people have dwelt on its shores—the "Nordic" Scandinavians and Germans, the Slavs, the "Baltic" Letts, Lithuanians and Old Prussians, and the Finno-Esths. Supremacy has been variable. In modern times, however, only one Baltic rivalry has been politically significant—the struggle of the growing Russians to keep a secure foothold on the Baltic, and the determination of Finns and Germans to prevent this. It is this common determination that has made these two latter peoples allies.

Germany's deft conquest of Norway and Denmark in 1940 was one of the first demonstrations of the weakness of navies without air support.

Thereby, the Baltic became inevitably a German lake. Could the Finno-German combination secure possession of Murmansk on the White Sea as well, the Soviets would be cut off from the western world here and driven back on the steppes. It

H Helsingör　　**Cux** Cuxhaven　　**W** Warnemünde　　**S** Sassnitz

was to prevent just such an incidence as this that early in World War Two the Soviet armies seized Hanko from the Finns and the three little countries of Esthonia, Latvia and Lithuania, with the excellent ports of Talinn, Riga and Liepaja.

It was to defend the Baltic Fleet at Kronstadt that the Soviets clung so stubbornly to nearby Leningrad.

To Germany, the Baltic is vital chiefly for one thing: from the Swedish mines near the head of the Gulf of Bothnia comes that ultraprecious iron ore that so lightens the task of the German supply manufacturers.

To the United Nations, the Baltic would seem unlikely to become vital save in the case British and Americans managed to recapture Norway and were seeking thereby to secure their sea and air communications with the Soviets across the Arctic Ocean, which might well require the occupation or elimination of Finland.

THE BLACK SEA

This second Russian "gill" is in size almost identical to the Baltic "gill" in the north (164,000 square miles). But it is shorter, plumper, and, except for the Crimea-Sea of Azov in the north, essentially regular. Looked at with Batum at the bottom, the Black Sea has the shape of a slightly distorted Africa. Incidentally, the Sea of Azov is so shallow it can properly be considered merely the inundated estuary of the River Don.

To oceanographers, the Black Sea is fascinating: its immensely deep waters—6000-7000 feet—contain, below the three-hundred-foot level, absolutely no organic life. The water is mildly salt; through the narrow channel into the Mediterranean runs on the surface an almost fresh-water current while down below heavily salted Mediterranean water pushes through into the Black Sea.

Climate is not greatly affected by the Black Sea: hot summers and cold winters are the rule. The only obstacles to navigation are the frequent severe tempests with cross winds. Ports are fairly frequent and towns have been common since Classical Greek days. The best modern harbors are Odessa, Poti and Batum, Trabzon (Trebizond) and Samsun.

For three hundred years the Black Sea, living up to its earliest Greek name of "inhospitable sea," was closed by the Turks to all but their own shipping. And in 1923 Turkey—subject to certain exceptions—was confirmed in control of the Straits. This gave the Turks power and plenty to worry about.

For these Straits are one of the most coveted international pivots on earth. Russia —Soviet or czarist—inevitably sought to force its way out of the back of the Black Sea antechamber at least into the corridor that is the Mediterranean. Britain opposed this surge, and Germany and, of course, Turkey. But meanwhile Germany developed a *Drang nach Osten* of its own across the Straits and to the Persian Gulf which crossed the Russian line more or less at right angles. Britain had hoped to utilize Greeks and Turks to thwart both Russians and Germans. But in World War Two hard-pressed Britain was glad of an understanding with Russia even, if need be, at cost of Turkish friendship. Turkey had even more to lose from Germans crashing through on their way to India than from Russians seeking a warm-water outlet to the Seven Oceans.

In the effort to preserve its neutrality in World War Two, Turkey sought to keep the Straits rigorously closed. This attitude left the Russian Black Sea Fleet the only halfway considerable naval force in these waters. So long as Russia could maintain an adequate base for this fleet, it could prevent an attack upon the oil districts of Maikop, Grozny and Baku from Georgia and Azerbaidzhan across the low Suram Pass (about 3500 feet). Germany therefore sought to drive the fleet along the coast from base to base until none was left. This was a terrific task and meanwhile the United States entered the war and started out-equipping the Germans and their Axis satellites.

Why the Germans did not first take over Turkey before attacking the Soviets was a problem that left strategists guessing. Once the Soviets were attacked and until they could be eliminated, any German attempt to do this was extremely hazardous, as was a correlated attempt to drive the British from Malta.

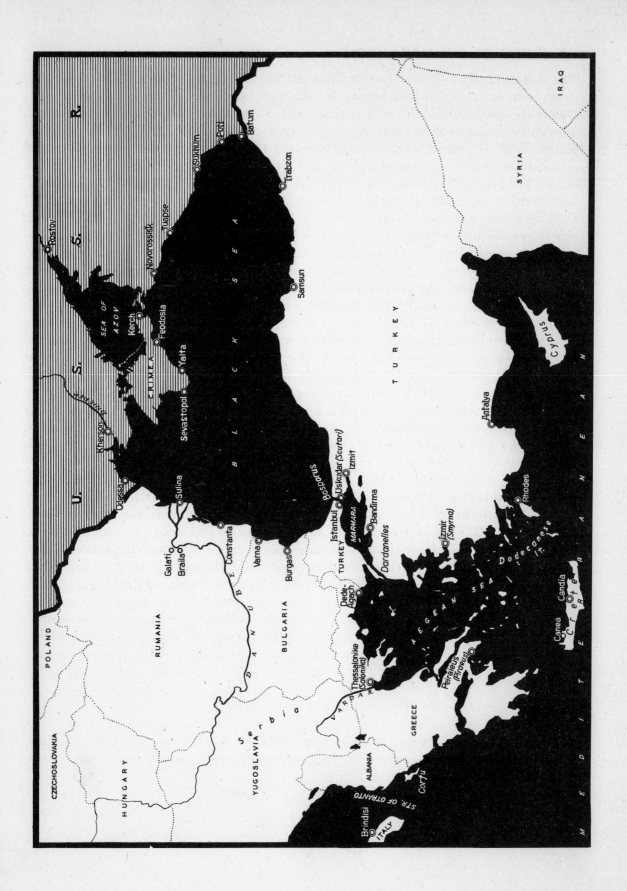

THE ROUTE OF THE VARANGERS

The Ancients put the boundary of "Europe" on the River Don. Historically it has more often been on the Dnieper. For it was approximately on the Dnieper line that essentially "western" Poles and Byzantine Greeks met and counterbalanced Crimean Tartars and other Mongols and only dubiously Occidental Muscovites. Further north, on the Dvina, Teutonic Knights and Polonized Lithuanians met strange fellows from the north and east, wrestled with them, and remained in a sort of equilibrium. There can be little doubt but that historically the Dnieper and the Dvina formed a boundary between one cultural world and another.

This would have been relatively simple but for another fact: mountains separate, but rivers unite. The Dnieper-Dvina line (with its alternative, the Dnieper-Loyat-Volkhov-Lake Ladoga route) constitutes the best waterway from the Black Sea to the Baltic. The Dniester-San-Vistula route is shorter—but leads through the hills. The way up the Prypec to the Bug and the Niemen is also shorter, but you must cross the difficult and dangerous Prypec marshes where an army can founder. Only the Dnieper-Dvina offers all the advantages—slow flowing, navigable waters on both sides with a relatively short portage between them. Therefore from time immemorial, the men of the south have used this road for their journeys north. From the south, from Byzantium, came Christianity and church cupola, Byzantine ikon and the civilized arts. Meanwhile, men of the North, the so-called Varangers who were probably Scandinavians, chose the same route to press southward, towards customers for their amber and furs, towards sunnier kingdoms to plunder and to conquer. From Stockholm to Istanbul, by far the most convenient route for traders went to Vitebsk and Smolensk or alternatively by Novgorod and Velikie Luki.

It is not much different today. This line is still the easiest between the two seas. In a war in this area, it is advantageous to have the Dnieper-Dvina line in one's rear. For further east, in the Soviet Union, distances expand and communications are long. Westward, the Prypec Marshes cut the territory in two and limit communications to the north and south. Here lies at least one reason why Hitler and the German generals so stubbornly clung to their advanced positions to the east during the hard winter of 1941-1942, even at cost of terrific suffering. Here is a reason why military authorities—in contrast to public opinion generally—considered that winter campaign as a strategical success for the Germans. For had the Soviet forces succeeded in forcing the Germans back upon this line and so "neutralizing" it, the Germans could not have launched a new west-east offensive without duplicating their terrific efforts (and losses) of 1941.

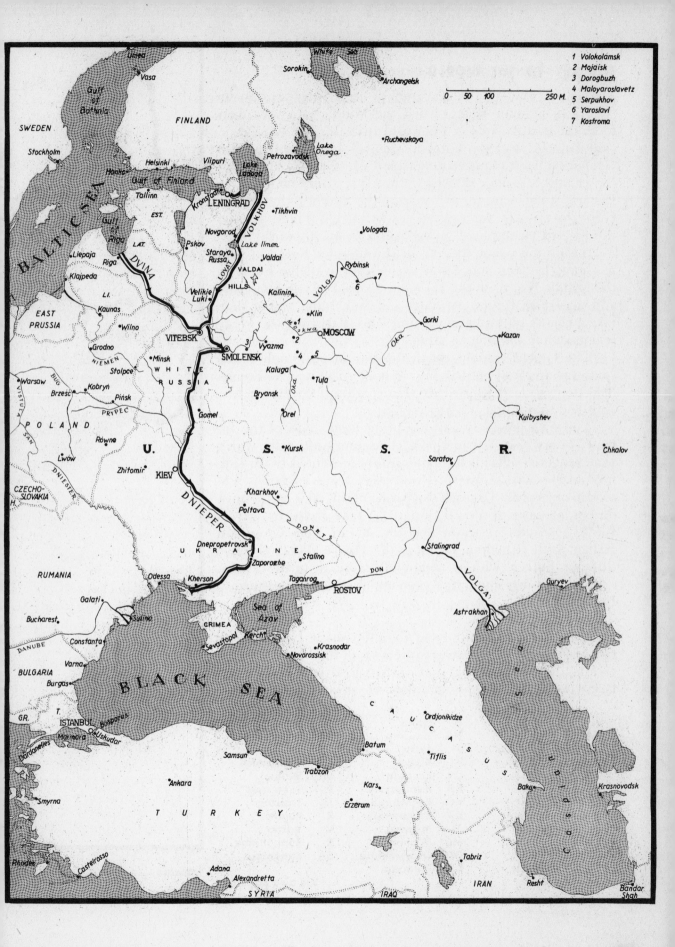

1 Volokolamsk
2 Mojaisk
3 Dorogbuzh
4 Maloyaroslavetz
5 Serpukhov
6 Yaroslavl
7 Kostroma

0   50   100   250 M.

SWEDEN

Gulf of Bothnia

FINLAND

Stockholm

Vasa

Umeå

Sorokin

Archangelsk

Ruchevskaya

BALTIC SEA

Helsinki
Hanko
Viipuri

Lake Ladoga

Petrozavodsk

Lake Onega

Gulf of Finland

Tallinn
Kronstadt
LENINGRAD

VOLKHOV

Tikhvin

Vologda

EST.

Novgorod

Gulf of Riga

Pskov

Staraya Russa

Lake Ilmen

Valdai

Rybinsk

7

LAT.

DVINA

LOVAT

VALDAI

6

Liepaja
Riga

Velikie Luki

HILLS

Kalinin

VOLGA

Klin

Gorki

Klajpeda

L.I.

Moskwa

MOSCOW

Kazan

EAST PRUSSIA

Kaunas

Wilno

VITEBSK

3

Vyazma

2

Oka

NIEMEN

Grodno

SMOLENSK

1

4   5

Kaluga

Tula

Gomel

Minsk

WHITE RUSSIA

Stolpce

Warsaw

BUG

Brzesc

Kobryn

Pinsk

PRYPEC

Bryansk

Orel

DON

Kuibyshev

POLAND

VISTULA

SAN

Rowne

U.   S.   S.   R.

Lwow

DNIESTER

Zhitomir

KIEV

Kursk

Saratov

Chkalov

CZECHO-SLOVAKIA

DNIEPER

Kharkhov

Poltava

DONETS

RUMANIA

Dnepropetrovsk

UKRAINE

Stalino

Stalingrad

VOLGA

Galati

Sulina

Zaporozhe

DON

Guryev

Bucharest

Odessa

Kherson

Taganrog

ROSTOV

Astrakhan

Constanta

CRIMEA

Sea of Azov

DANUBE

Varna

Sevastopol

Kerch

Krasnodar

BULGARIA

Burgas

Novorossisk

CAUCASUS

BLACK   SEA

GR.
T.

ISTANBUL
Uskudar

Bosporus

Ordjonikidze

Marmara

Dardanelles

Samsun

Batum

Tiflis

Baku

Rhodes

Ankara

Trabzon

Kars

Krasnovodsk

Smyrna

TURKEY

Erzerum

Tabriz

Castelrosso

IRAN

Resht

Adana

Alexandretta

SYRIA

IRAQ

Bandar Shah

93

THE KEY TO THE WORLD

A scientist who, in the Autumn of 1940, suggested to an American Cabinet Member that the Middle East was likely to be the decisive area in the world struggle, met amused incredulity. Yet had the Cabinet Member been familiar with *Geopolitik* he would have understood why German ambitions center in this region. He who holds the territory between the Eastern Mediterranean, the Aegean, the Red Sea, the Persian Gulf, the Caspian Sea and the Black Sea, has a tight grip on the Eastern Hemisphere, and conceivably on the world.

It is for this reason that the British Cabinet, forced in 1941 to choose between concentrating its scant available forces in the Middle East or in the Far East, decided to risk Singapore and the Dutch Indies, Australia and even India, rather than take a chance on losing Egypt and Suez, Palestine, the Mesopotamian and the Iranian oil fields.

The United Nations began the war in possession of the contested area and needed only to hold on to it. The French defection seriously jeopardized their position. But to win, the Axis had to conquer this key region.

The Axis possessed a strong bridgehead south of the Inland Waterway in Italian Libya, communications with which were rendered difficult but not entirely prevented by British-held Malta. Axis seizure of Crete offset United Nations possession of Cyprus. To reach the coveted goal, Axis forces must do one or more of several things: (1) take Egypt by way of Libya; (2) seize Syria and Palestine by air from Crete and Italian Rodi (Rhodes); (3) cross the Dardanelles and move through Turkey, with or without the consent of the Turks; (4) push through southern Russia and the high Caucasus into Iraq or Iran.

No one was easy.

Reinforcing and supplying their forces in Libya in the face of United Nations naval supremacy in the Mediterranean entailed heavy losses. And once in North Africa, the invaders faced the terrific supply problem of advancing across the

Railways ═══ 5'0" gauge ═══ 4'8½" g[auge]

A	Abadan	H	Homs	U	Ulukisla		
AH	Ahwaz	HA	Haditha	S	Sulina		
AL	Alexandretta	J	Julfa	SH	Shiraz		
AL F	Al Falluja	K	Kizlyar	Sar	Sarikamish		
AS	Astara	KA	Karbala	ST	Stalino		
BJ	Borazjan	KD	Kandagach	T	Taganrog		
B	Burgas	KO	Koshchagil	TR	Trabzon		
BO	Boghazkeny	KR	Krasnodar	R	Rayak		
C	Constanta	M	Mersina	V	Varna		
CH	Charshemoe	MA	Mianeh	Z	Zongouldak		
CI	Cizre	O	Ordjonikidze	ZA	Zaporozhe		
D	Diyarbekir	P	Palmyra				

See also page 67.

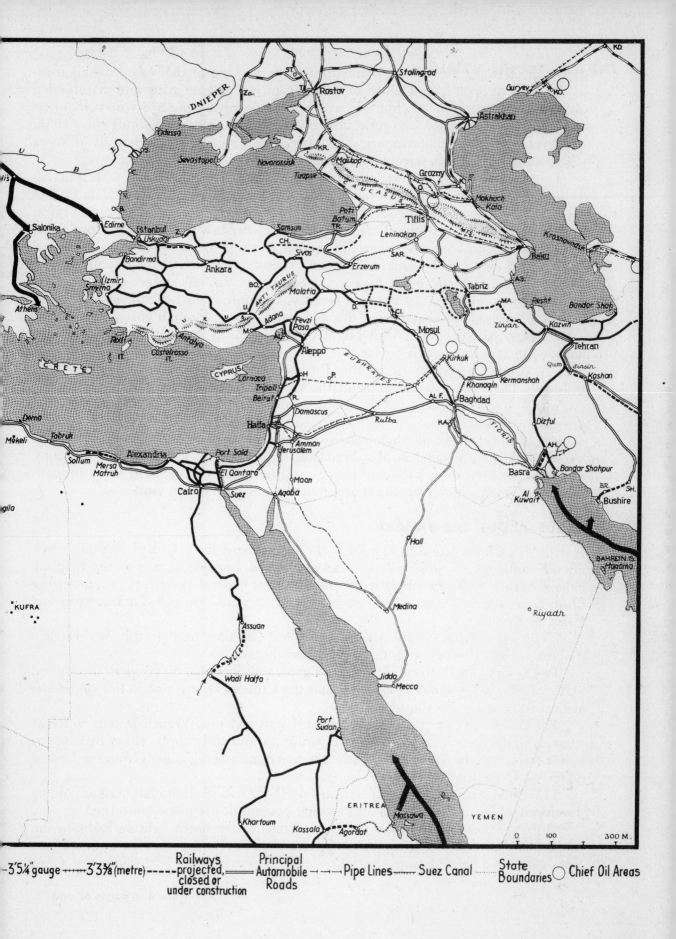

desert, or of facing air and sea bombardment by sticking to the only (coastal) road.

Invasion of Syria from Crete and Rodi meant not only securing and maintaining complete mastery of the air, but also sending and supplying many divisions by plane alone, during a campaign that promised to last until the United Nations Navy could be driven from the Mediterranean altogether. The United Nations base at Massawa was too distant to be effectively bombarded.

The most tempting plan for the Axis was to pass through Turkey with Turkish consent. But the position of German-ridden Hungary, Bulgaria, Roumania or Slovakia held nothing attractive for free Turks, who seemed sure to remain neutral as long as they dared. Were the Turks to fight, they could, with United Nations assistance, put up stubborn resistance. Turkey is a rough country, mountainous and barren, with extremes of climate. The main railroad from Istanbul through Ankara, Boghazkeny, Adana and Fevzi Pasa to Aleppo passes through gorges easy to defend and over bridges easy to cast down. The alternate route from Boghazkeny to Samsun and Erzerum leads ultimately to Tiflis and Baku, but it is tough going.

Southern Russia bristles with obstacles even without the added annoyance of a hostile Russian army and a Soviet fleet protecting one flank of the Caucasus—accessible to the north and south by the Tuapse-Tiflis and the Rostov-Makhach Kala railroads. The region to the south of the Caspian is one of the most unhealthy in the world. Even from Baku, Axis troops would find access to Mesopatamia or Iran distinctly difficult.

But if the Axis faced grave offensive problems, defense of the region by the United Nations was not less of a headache, if only for reason of communications. With the Mediterranean closed to convoys, all men and supplies had to be brought many thousands of miles by ship to the Red Sea and the Persian Gulf.

LANDS ABOUT THE SAHARA

North Africa from Morocco to Suez is the springboard for a United Nations attack on the southern or "soft" side of Axis-dominated Europe. It is also the first-line defense against an Axis south drive across the Great Central Waterway, whether from Spain across the Strait, from Italy into Libya or overland through Turkey, Syria and Palestine to Suez.

West Africa, from Casablanca to Dakar and Conakry, and notably Spanish Rio de Oro, is the "air key" to both Atlantic Oceans.

The Sahara Desert, from Morocco to Egypt, and one-sixth bigger than the United States (total area 3,500,000 square miles), is the United Nations second line of defense against Axis expansion southward.

The "waist" of Africa, say from British Lagos and Free French Douala to Khartoum, is a vital line of United Nations communications and supply, either by plane or motor truck, and the shortest route (the Mediterranean being closed) from the United States and Great Britain to Cairo.

Therefore, during the present war, this northern half of Africa has been amazingly developed so far as land routes and ground communications are concerned.

Along the coast, and notably in eastern Libya where much fighting has gone on, numerous roads not shown on this map have been developed—they go nowhere save from a base to a fighting front. But other more important ones lead southward across

See also pages 67 and 71.

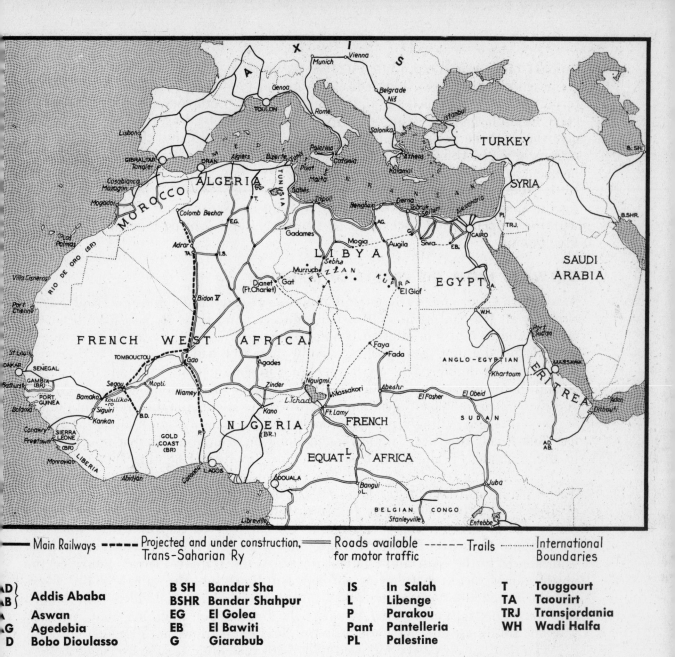

| | Main Railways | -----| Projected and under construction, Trans-Saharian Ry | =====| Roads available for motor traffic | ------| Trails | ....| International Boundaries |

the Sahara from nearly every important center. Many of the routes shown as simple tracks on the map opposite can be used by motor vehicles with special tires. A large part of the Sahara is terrible sand—the worst example of soil erosion in the world. But much of it is high—the Tibesti Highland rises to 8000 ft.—and consists of stony wastes called *hammada* which support motor traffic easily. With water, gasoline and food supplies distributed about the desert, with men more or less everywhere, this country has in part lost its former inaccessibility and terror. True, it remains hot—at Azizia in south Tripolitania the highest natural temperature on the earth's surface has been recorded—136 degrees Fahrenheit in the shade. But Sahara nights are cool save in summer. And even in summer fighting can continue.

From the United Nations viewpoint the most important route is that across the "waist" from Douala to Bangui, Ft. Lamy, Abeshr and the Nile. Here pass the precious supplies. The Axis is more interested in the progress of the French Trans-Saharan Railway southward from the Mediterranean and branching into four arms to reach terminals at Dakar, Conakry, Abdjan and Cotonou. Completion of this—started by good Republicans but continued with Nazi approval by Vichy Frenchmen—could give the Axis the possibility of pouring men and supplies into these West African terminals, of blocking the airlines and sealines across the South Atlantic, and of menacing Brazil.

It should not be forgotten, however, that the opening of this railroad, scheduled for the Spring of 1943, might just as well mean its eventual use, not by Axis forces with the cooperation of Vichy, but by United Nations fighting men in the name of Free France.

OUTWARD FROM THE CRADLE OF MANKIND

Asia west of China and north of the mountains—Himalayas, Pamirs and Hindukush— is nearly all Russian or under Russian influence. And these steppes have been the greatest known source of migrant peoples. During thousands of years there regularly went forth tribe after tribe, pushing against those that had gone before it.

From here the ancestors of the present Chinese—and of mankind—first started several thousand years before the Christian era. One group swept across Manchuria and then down into Shantung. Another crossed the low mountains from Gobi to the region of Peiping. Still others, more numerous, came slanting down along the almost flat "Silk Road" from Russian Turkestan along the same route as that now followed by the thousands of camels and trucks bringing supplies for fighting China.

Far more numerous were the tribes that migrated westward across the endless Tartar plains to Russia, or turning south of the Thian Shan, crossed the pass north of Kashgar into the valley of the Jaxartes. Here their road turned south around the end of the Hindukush and divided. One branch swerved sharply to the southeast and led into India over the Khyber Pass. The other bent southwest through Baluchistan almost to the coast and climbed up across the Iranian Plateau following the northwesterly valleys that emerge through Kurdistan into the valleys of the Tigris and the Euphrates. Near what is now Mosul, the road again divided. One branch continued northwest across Asia Minor to the Dardanelles; the other bent gradually west and southwest into Syria and Palestine, and swung down into Egypt.

Who shall say why tribe followed tribe with incredible regularity? Some believe it was pressure from a highly populated poor land into a relatively empty richer one. But that does not explain it. For while some vagrant peoples were admittedly sucked into vacuums, others moved into thickly inhabited country and made the needed vacuum with the sword. Occasionally the movement stopped or went into a brief period of reverse.

Each of these tribes generally drove some other beaten peoples before it and was itself pushed on or overrun. This was the great *Voelkerwanderung* that seems so romantic to German scholars in search of explanations why Germany should take the earth.

For modern strategy the point is as follows:

The world is again on the move. Wherever primitive tribes, on foot, on horse or

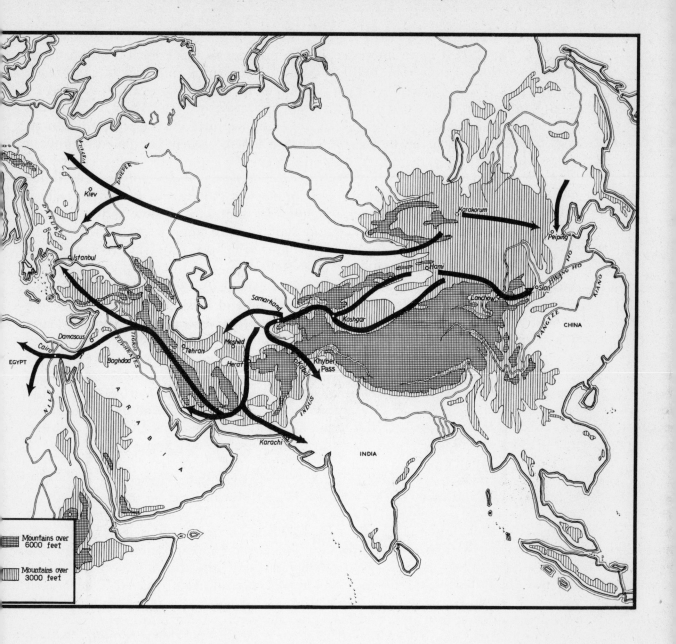

in carts could pass, it is relatively easy for modern motor transport, with some aid from the roadbuilders, to follow them. Before the end of this war, each of the ancient routes may have been built out into broad ultra-modern highways along which tanks and motorized divisions may sweep under a protective cloud of hornets.

The Nazi aim is clearly to cut Europe and Africa from Asia and then crash through Iraq, Iran and Baluchistan to meet Japanese allies in India. United Nations will necessarily do anything possible to prevent this: and if they fail, they will utilize their central position and inner communications on the Russian side to try to cut the German lines. In this effort they will, almost with mathematical certainty, follow the ancient tracks of the vagrant tribesmen of Central Asia.

INDIA

India's future is potentially as overwhelming as its past. Strategically, its present is enigmatic.

Look first at its situation. Here is a promontory projected southward into the Indian Ocean. As a naturally rich, highly developed, densely populated country, it exercised a vast influence outside its own territory. The "rupee area" included portions of Africa and Arabia, as well as Burma, Thailand and parts of the East Indies. Indian merchants are scattered throughout the world as far as Gibraltar and the Caribbean: Britain established special rights for Indians in Kenya and at Zanzibar and in the Fiji Islands. Indian trade and manufactures were potent all through the Middle East, in Tibet and across the Himalayas in faraway Sinkiang. Its ports, Bombay, Madras, Calcutta, are admirably situated for commerce in every direction. India's extension, Ceylon, occupies the key strategic position in the Indian Ocean. India is bordered by Iran, Afghanistan, Soviet Russia, Tibet, China and Burma.

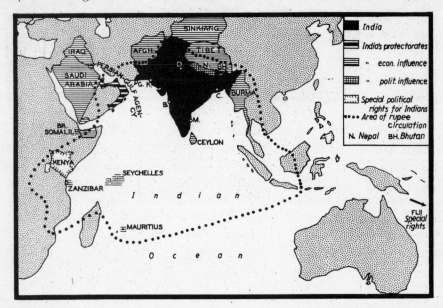

Then consider its physical features. In the north the highest mountains in the world all but isolate it from its neighbors in that direction. Two great river valleys, the Indus and the Ganges, comprise more than half its territory. Between them is the dry, hot Thar desert. In the south stretches the high plateau called the Deccan, ascent to which is over palisade-like mountains, the Ghats. In the east, where the Ganges and Brahmaputra join, is a rich, steaming delta country, Bengal. Here in India are not only the highest mountains but the broadest plains, the most torrid heat, the most torrential rains anywhere on this planet.

This country, just over half as large as the United States, is inhabited by approximately three times the people, or six times as many per square mile. One out of every five persons on earth is an Indian. Eighty-nine percent of them are rural and inhabit 700,000 villages, or almost one village per two square miles. Inevitably they are poor and probably eighty percent illiterate. They speak 222 different languages or dialects,

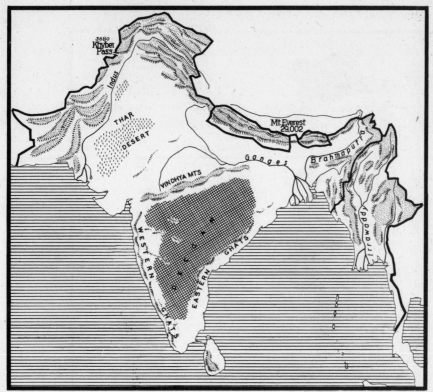

are divided into many religions and sub-religions (which they take seriously) and possess one cow for each two people, or approximately two hundred million cows, all of them sacred, and most of them an economic liability.

Indians normally import rice for food but export jute, the only substance which can be made up into sacks in which rice for export will not "sweat" and spoil. They produce a large amount of cotton. Iron mines are fairly extensive; there is some oil and a good deal of valuable manganese, with chromium and gold. There is a considerable steel and textile industry and—lately developed—war factories.

Britain invested nearly a billion pounds in India and took about a third of India's exports. Indians are intelligent. They make good craftsmen and aviators, but show little enthusiasm for a military career.

The country has fair roads, good telegraphs, and the fourth largest railway system (this last divided into three separate gauges).

Yet as the country is disunited religiously and linguistically, so is it a political hodge-podge. Still actually ruled—despite local self-government—by about a thousand Civil Servants (John Gunther in 1938 found that only 591 were British) and "protected" by a few score thousand troops split between the "British Army in India" and the "Indian Army," the Administration has room for two sorts of Provinces and 522 independent Native States, each of these latter with its local army. Most of the educated Hindus wished full independence from Britain, or claimed to. Most of the Moslem fourth of the people preferred British rule to rule by Hindus, but some wanted to secede and join Moslem Afghanistan just over the Northwest Frontier.

To oppose the Japanese—whom most intelligent Indians undoubtedly feared and disliked—half a million first-class, well-equipped soldiers were necessary. India could supply that many soldiers easily, but equipment and air support might be lacking.

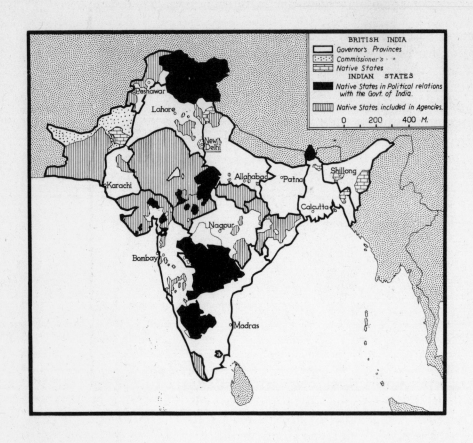

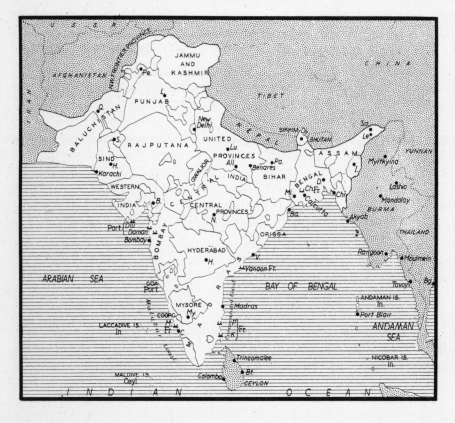

All	Allahabad
B	Baroda
Ba	Balasor
Bg	Bangkok
Bt	Batticaloa
C	Calicut
Ch	Chandernagor
Chi	Chittagong
D	Dacca
Dj	Darjeeling
H	Hyderabad
I	Imphal (Manipur)
K	Karikal
L	Lahore
Le	Ledo
Lu	Lucknow
M	Mahe
Mi	Midnapur
My	Mysore
N	Nagpur
P	Pondichery
Pa	Parna
Pe	Peshawar
Q	Quetta
S	Sukkur
Sa	Sadiya
V	Vizagapatan

Two excellent naval bases, Bombay and Trincomalee, if well defended, offered an adequate foundation for naval defense. But nothing can ever substitute for adequate morale and (in June 1942) none knew whether the Indian masses had any. If they had, no available Japanese army could fight its way through India. If they had none, then Japan's task might be achieved merely by the occupation of Calcutta (from which to destroy the circumambient war industries), Trincomalee and Bombay. In other words, the strategy of Indian defense was partly a matter of psychology.

Westerners felt sure that the resolute "non-violent, non-cooperation" which Mohandas Gandhi promised to oppose to the Japanese, though not unsuccessful against conscience-ridden British, was unlikely to make a dent on hard-boiled Japanese.

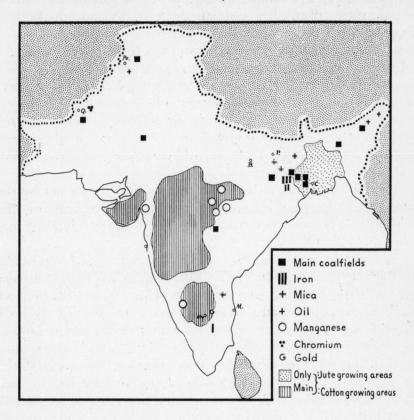

LAND AND SEA GATES TO CHINA

China is an immense country. But the densely populated part, often called China proper is an area bounded on the north by Peiping-Kalgan and on the west, roughly, by a line drawn through Lanchow, Chengtu and Kunming. This is in normal times a reasonably accessible territory. From Tsingtao to Canton are twenty good sea ports. A railway enters the country from Korea. Another drops down on Peiping from Manchuria. A third pokes up to Kunming from Hanoi in French Indo China. So much for front entrances. There are in addition at least three back entrances. From Ulan Ude in Siberia a road leads to Ulan Bator in Russian-protected Outer Mongolia. Further it does not go, but the desert is hard and except in the rainy season you can drive a car without too much difficulty from Ulan Bator to Kalgan and Peiping. Another track—the famous Silk Road—leads from Lanchow right across semi-deserted country by Ansi, Hami, and Tihwa to enter Siberia and reach Sergiopol on the Soviet Turk-Sib Railroad. A dirt track was developed into the Burma Road.

There are no other motor routes leading into China. Yet trails accessible to nothing heavier than man or mule exist in many places. The most notable lead from Chengtu up into Tibet and from Sadiya in Upper Assam over high mountains to Hanyuang and Sichang, respectively, on the highway from Siangyun on the Burma Road to Chengtu. But they are only tracks and incredible labor is necessary to make them into something that can carry a motorcar.

By June 1942, all China's gateways but one had been blocked by the Japanese. The blockade of the China ports was completed in May of that year after the American air raid on Tokyo; the Japanese determined to occupy all of China that might provide airfields within a reasonable distance of Japan.

The Korean entrance was seized back in the Nineties of the last century; the South Manchurian Railway in 1931. The Indo China line in 1940-1941. Burma was taken in the Spring of 1942. Nothing was left to the Chinese but the old Silk Road to Soviet Russia. This was developed into an excellent route for motors, open nearly all the year round. But its excessive length made motor traffic almost impractical, since cars consumed in a round trip as much fuel as they could carry. Camels brought the gas to make up the deficiency. Like time, they were sure but "exceeding slow."

Nothing, that is, but the untracked ways of the air. Air freight had long been considered a perfectly feasible and indeed a paying proposition. Nowhere had it been properly developed until the need for keeping China open more or less forced the United Nations leaders to divert a number of carriers to the India-China line. President Roosevelt promised that China would receive supplies. American General Stilwell insisted that lost Burma must be reconquered.

See also page 16.

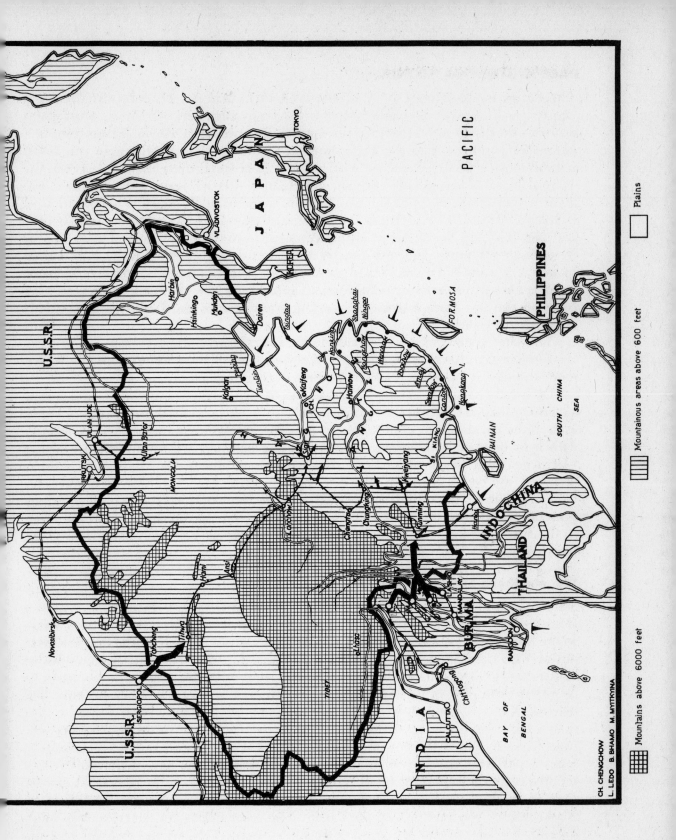

PACIFIC

JAPAN

TOKYO

KOREA

VLADIVOSTOK

Harbin

Hsinkingo

Mukden

Dairen

Tsingtao

U.S.S.R.

IRKUTSK

ULAN UDE

Ulan Bator

MONGOLIA

Kalgan

Peiping

Tientsin

Shanghai

Ningpo

FORMOSA

Kaifeng

Hankow

Changsha

Foochow

Amoy

SOUTH
CHINA
SEA

PHILIPPINES

Sian

Chengtu

Kweiyang

Canton

Hongkong

Novosibirsk

Chunking

Kunming

KIANG

HAINAN

INDOCHINA

Lanchow

Cheng

SERGIOPOL

Tihwa

Tacheng

TIBET

Lhasa

Hami

Ansi

THAILAND

Hanoi

BURMA

M.
B.
L.

CALCUTTA

Chittagong

RANGOON

BAY
OF
BENGAL

INDIA

CH. CHENGCHOW
L. LEDO   B. BHAMO   M. MYITKYINA

⊞ Mountains above 6000 feet

▥ Mountainous areas above 600 feet

☐ Plains

105

PACIFIC STEPPING STONES

The Pacific is the greatest body of water on earth and not properly divisible into "north" and "south." In the southwest, a sunken continent of which Australia is probably the rump, forms what has poetically been called the "Pacific Mediterranean." This phrase is one key to the understanding of the Pacific. For although this ocean is enormous (from the Philippines to Ecuador is nearly eleven thousand miles), the western half is so plentifully strewn with islands that navigating the seas between them has always been no more adventurous than the island-to-island navigation of Grecian Odysseus. There are thousands and thousands of them. Some, like Borneo and New Guinea, are as big as whole countries; most are just dots. There are, for instance, two hundred and fifty isles included in the single group of the Fijis. Lured by ever new islands, Polynesians in giant canoes, sometimes lashed together in pairs, became the earth's earliest ocean sailors. Considering that their ancestors may have come all the way from Europe by crossing two-thirds of the Pacific, they certainly set a mark as travellers.

The same islands which beckoned them, lure the modern aggressor.

This broken character of the western and notably of the southwestern Pacific has tended to give a brand new character to warfare.

Destroyers, cruisers, perhaps a battleship or two, precede, surround, and follow a convoy of troop carrying transports, ammunition and supply ships. Ahead of them, high in the air, the scout planes fan out over the isle-strewn waters. Airplane carriers with light bombers and fighters follow. Heavier bombers and troop-carrying planes —hardened parachutists—wait at the nearest base. As fast as an island flying field is occupied, the bombers and troop planes push forward, land, establish a rudimentary base and wait for the next hop. Steadily, but on the whole successfully, the strange procession advances. It is tri-elemental war—in the air, on the sea and on the land. And because the distances between the Pacific islands are relatively short, this is the ideal country for this totally new kind of warfare.

The Northern Stepping Stones

Start at Japan and go north. The chain of tiny Kurile islands that Japan acquired from Russia back in the Seventies of the last century stretch like a barrier right across to the Kamchatka peninsula, closing off the Okhotsk Sea. Nearly at the northern end of the chain is Paramushiro, reputed a formidable Japanese base. From Paramushiro to Russian Petropavlovsk is 220 statute miles. Here turn east, and from this latter to American Attu, first of the Aleutians, is 610 miles. There is not much on Attu. But inviting Kiska is not far. From American Kiska to Japanese Paramushiro is less than a thousand miles. From Kiska to Tokyo is 2000 miles. In the other direction, from Kiska to Dutch Harbor on Unalaska Island it is only 672 miles. Unalaska possesses a powerful naval base. Beyond Unalaska Island you have Unimak Passage, reputed the most important bit of water in this area, for this is the only good eastern channel between Bering Sea and American Pacific waters. Here the mainland of Alaska begins: you have crossed the Pacific. The other important American bases and stations—Kodiak, Anchorage (with Fort Richardson), head of the railroad to Fairbanks, Seward, head of the Richardson Highway to the same place, Fairbanks itself with its cold weather experimental station, Sitka close to Canada—these are mainland affairs. Between Sitka and Japan—or better, between Seattle and Japan, the final stage of the Pacific war may be waged. Properly to carry the air war to Japan, the Americans

See also pages 39, 45, 49, 53 and 55.

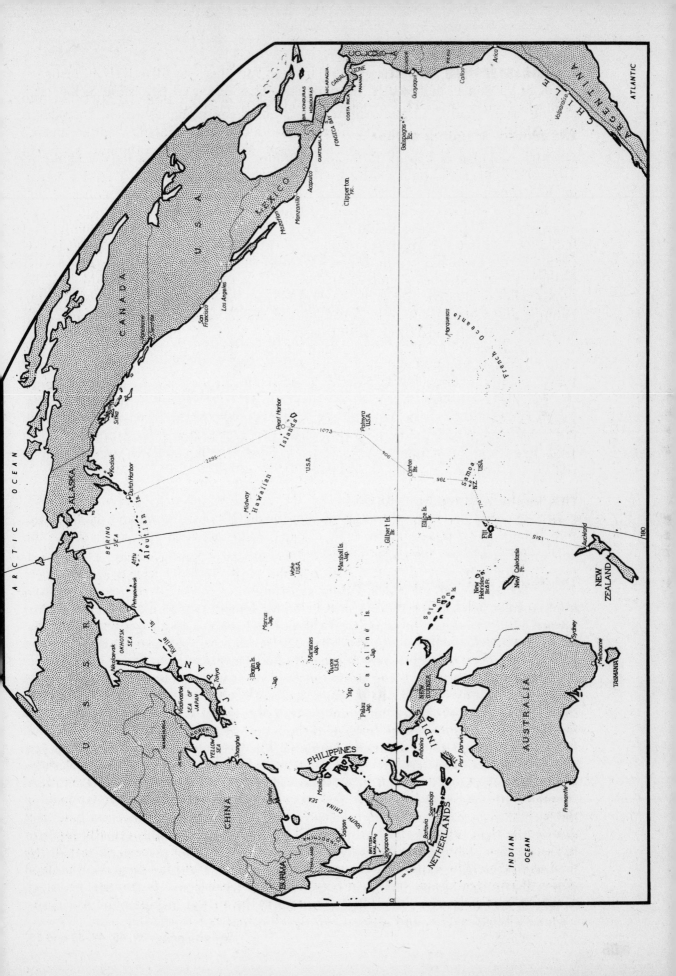

should have Russian Petropavlovsk or Japanese Paramushiro. Effectively to bring air terror to Vancouver and Seattle, the Japanese absolutely need possession of Kodiak—or maybe even of Sitka. This struggle, too, will be tri-elemental.

The Middle Stepping Stones

Go back to Japan and drop southeast to Bonin Island. Here you have a choice of directions. You can keep on south into the Marianas until you touch Japanese Saipan or the (temporarily lost) American possession of Guam. Then proceed southeast and you hit the Carolinas, with the Japanese bases of Truk, Ponape and Jaluit. Not far away is the tiny phosphate island of (British) Nauru. But ahead at a thousand and ten miles, you face the American outposts of Howland and Baker Islands and before trying to take them and get on to Pearl Harbor, eight hundred and twenty-five miles farther, you stop and bring up reinforcements. If you took these, you would come up square against another group of Anglo-American outposts: Palmyra, Washington, Fanning and Christmas Islands. And here the islands cease: there is little but deep water between you and Lower California.

Go back to Bonin. Had you turned southeast two hops of seven hundred and eighty and eight hundred and sixty miles, respectively, would let you examine scarred Wake, where the American Marines took their toll of heavy Japanese material until the last plane was shot down. From Wake to Midway Island (still following the Pacific Clipper route) is the trifle of 1185 miles and from there to Pearl Harbor 1304 miles made more easy by the long thin chain of the Hawaiians. At Midway early in June 1942, combined American forces made hash of a Japanese armada coming to take over the place and move on to Honolulu.

The Southern Stepping Stones

Start once more in Japan and work yourself down across the Ryukyu Islands to the Philippines. From Davao hop to New Guinea. From there, if you are man enough, you might reach the Solomons, close to the southern stepping stones. These reach from Australia by way of New Caledonia, the New Hebrides, the storied Fijis, to French Society Islands (of which Tahiti is the best known)—in all, over four thousand miles, the last hop to Papeete on Tahiti being the longest (1420 miles). Beyond Tahiti toward South America, the islands get thinner and then cease altogether. Just as the northeastern Pacific, inside the Hawaiian Islands, the southeastern Pacific is almost bare of land over an area as vast as the Atlantic Ocean.

Worth remembering: flying boats can land on lagoons at nearly all these larger islands and on hundreds of smaller ones, landing fields have mostly to be made but the difficulties are generally not immense. Small vessels can often find shelter; submarine supply stations can be hidden in thousands of places.

This is Oceania and the earthly Paradise. The weather is warm with sea breezes and plentiful rains. There are many good harbors for large ships. In many cases, troop carrying planes can jump from island to island without extending themselves.

One could argue, as has Major Seversky, that longer range bombers are making the battleship an anachronism and the carrier a dodo. Admittedly airplanes sink ships more easily than ships shoot down planes. Land-based fighters are normally superior to carrier-based fighters. Almost surely flyers will play a more important part in the final score than many sailors are yet ready to admit. But it will not be air power alone that will win, but teamwork. Heavy war material has still to be brought by ocean freighter. Probable victor: the side that can build ships faster and protect them better —whose soldiers, sailors and airmen can develop together the better team.

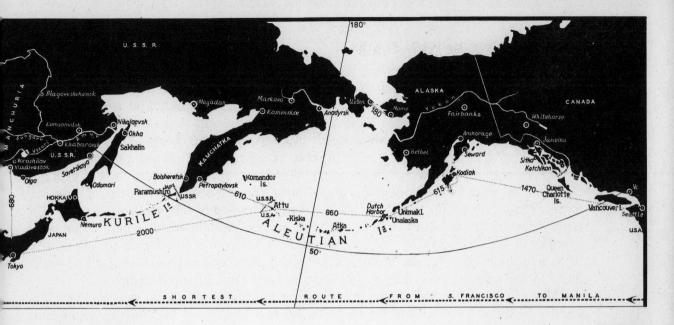

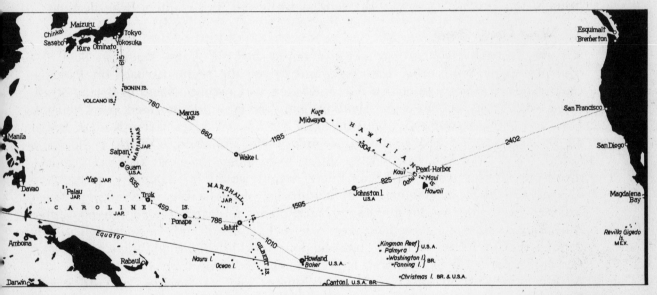

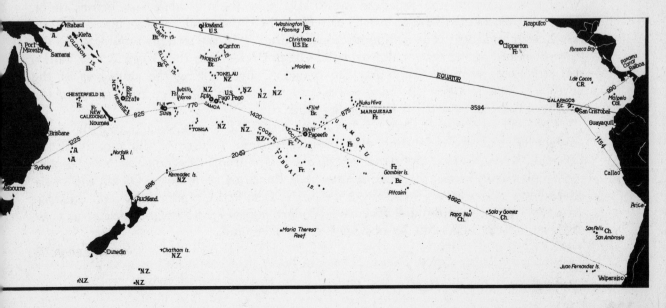

INVADING THE UNITED STATES

Strategically, continental United States is relatively easy to defend against attack from the sea. The Pacific approaches to the country are difficult, but only so long as Alaska, Hawaii, Lower California and the Panama Canal are held. The three thousand mile long frontier with Canada is extremely vulnerable and so is the Gulf of Mexico, with the natural gate of the Mississippi. Hudson Bay and the St. Lawrence River valley invite invasion by any power capable of seizing Iceland and Greenland.

Weaknesses in American defense at the beginning of the war were lack of strategical thinking and lack of offensive spirit, both of which led to neglect of fighting forces. Most Americans, until catapulted into a war they felt was coming but did nearly everything to avoid, had thought of strategy as something alien to them, a product of old Europe with its "eternal wars." Ability to forget that in the course of its national existence, the United States has fought as many wars as any European State in the same period, might well have proved fatal to the country.

More appropriate than most American monuments would be one to the "Unknown Japanese" responsible for the decision to attack Pearl Harbor, an attack that brought the United States into the conflict while the Axis could still be beaten.

1. West Coast Gaps

Suppose that the Japanese had met and vanquished all of the American fleet that could be spared from other waterways and driven the remnants back on Panama, California and Puget Sound; that they had taken St. Lawrence Island in Bering Strait, taken over Alaska, occupied the Aleutians from the land side, stormed Pearl Harbor. How would the Japanese go about invading the United States? From Kodiak Island off Alaska to Seattle is about 1500 statute miles; from Honolulu to Seattle 2774 statute miles, to San Francisco 2408 statute miles. Even along the new Alaskan Highway, the overland trek from Alaska to Puget Sound would be—against a determined opposition with at least equality of land-based planes—a big undertaking. Much easier an attempt by sea. Pit long-range battle planes and carrier-based fighters against American land-based fighters, and try to seize Esquimault and Bremerton bases by direct assault. Whether or not it could be done would depend, doubtless, upon what was at this point left of American fighting forces and American morale.

But even with Seattle's naval establishments and air factories and the Pacific Northwest occupied, the Japanese would still have their greatest task before them. This map shows all the flat, low level regions of the coastal zone in black. All the rest is high and most of it is mountainous. Rather than try to fight their way up the Columbia and Snake Rivers and over the Great Divide into the Green River Valley, real strategists seem to think that the invaders, after seizing the shipyards of the northwest, would follow the coast southward and try to seize San Francisco and the Southern California airplane factories by land.

The next step—rather than the hard trip across the Sierra-Nevada and the desert —might logically be a landing in Lower California, seizure of the mouth of the Colorado River, a rapid motorized advance across southern Arizona and New Mexico to the plains of Texas, the Rio Grande and the Gulf of Mexico. Of all the transcontinental routes across the United States, the Gila-Rio Grande is the only one that virtually side-steps mountain obstacles. Modern motor-cum-airplane tactics measure distance, not by miles but by obstacles to be overcome.

See also page 75.

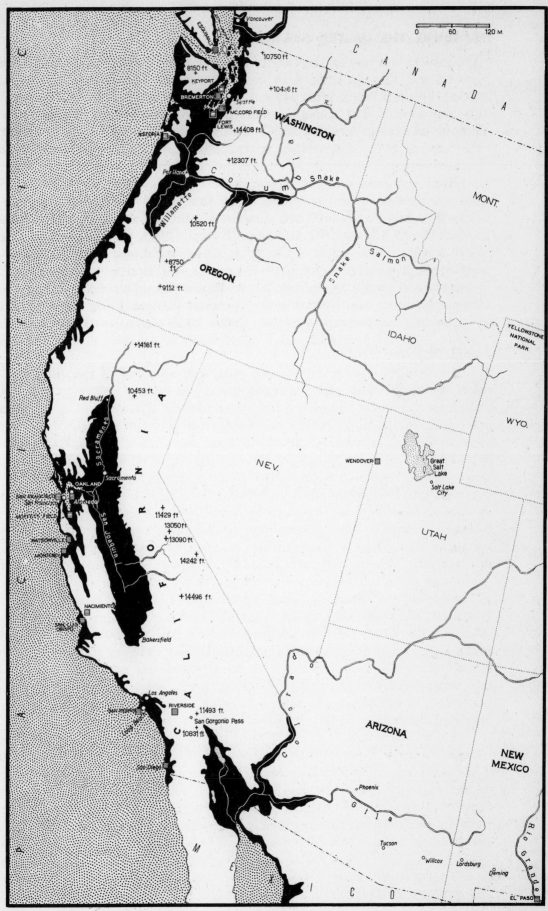

k indicates
ns and areas
o 500 feet alti-
. To the east of
e are shown
cipal highest
mits of the
ra Nevada
ifornia) and
ade Range (N.
fornia and
hington).
quares with
zontal shading
military bases.

0   60   120 M.

CANADA

Vancouver

+10750 ft.

ESQUIMALT

8150 ft.
+
KEYPORT

+104·6 ft.

BREMERTON

Seattle

WASHINGTON

MC.CORD FIELD

FORT
LEWIS

+14408 ft.

ASTORIA

+12307 ft.

Columbia

Snake

MONT.

Portland

Willamette

Snake

Salmon

+10520 ft.

OREGON

+8750 ft.

+9112 ft.

IDAHO

YELLOWSTONE
NATIONAL
PARK

+14161 ft.

C   A   L   I   F   O   R   N   I   A

Red Bluff

10453 ft.
+

Sacramento

NEV.

WENDOVER

WYO.

Great
Salt
Lake

OAKLAND

Sacramento

San Francisco
San Francisco
Alameda

MOFFETT FIELD

11429 ft.
+

13050 ft.
+
+13090 ft.

San Joaquin

Salt Lake
City

UTAH

+
14242 ft.

MONTEREY

+14496 ft.

NACIMIENTO

SAN LUIS
OBISPO

Bakersfield

Colorado

Los Angeles

RIVERSIDE

+ 11493 ft.

ARIZONA

NEW
MEXICO

SAN PEDRO

San Gorgonio Pass
+
10831 ft.

Long Beach

San Diego

Phoenix

Gila

M   E

X   I   C   O

Tucson

Willcox

Lordsburg

Rio Grande

Deming

EL PASO

P   A   C   I   F   I   C

2. The Mississippi-Missouri Valley

The vital center of the United States is the Mississippi Valley. The easiest entrance is upstream from the Gulf of Mexico. Therefore a Pacific Ocean invader, like Japan, rather than attack our West Coast first, might be tempted to have a go at the Panama Canal in a bold effort to reach the Gulf of Mexico by sea (though the locks and Gatun Dam would surely be dynamited). An Atlantic invader would normally start with the Gulf of Mexico, probably seizing Miami, Key West and Tampa for bases as he came along.

Next only to the valley of the Amazon, the Mississippi-Missouri Valley is the greatest river basin in the world. From New Orleans to Duluth—indeed to Hudson Bay—from Pittsburgh to Denver, there are no serious obstacles. The country is webbed with railroads and concrete highways. Water courses, though abundant, are generally slow flowing. Only a few of the many rivers are broad enough to embarrass army engineers. And—most important!—here is the vital center of the United States. Union possession of Vicksburg and the Lower Mississippi split the Confederacy. Axis possession of St. Louis and Detroit would do more than anything else to scotch American defense. Were invaders from New Orleans to join hands with invaders from Hudson Bay or the Saint Lawrence, the United States, to all intents and purposes, would be whipped.

Fortunately for Americans, the great central valley is naturally one of the best defended regions on earth, and the hardest to invade.

See also page 39.

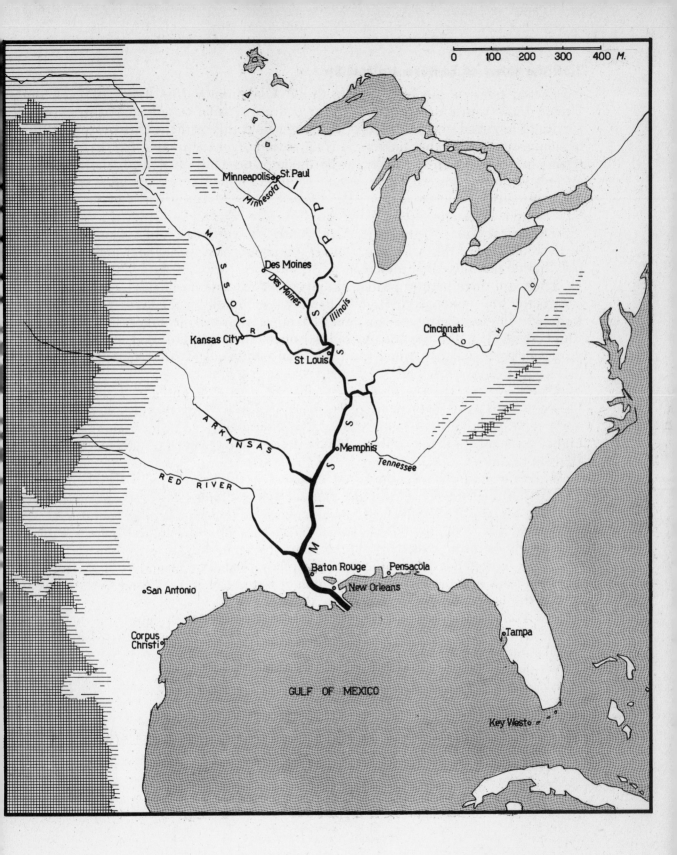

3. Rivergates of Eastern United States

No enemy, however numerous, could think of landing on the eastern coast of the United States with murderous intent that had not secured command of the sea and air. Raids intended to destroy this or that city or put this or that industrial sector out of commission are another matter. So is the action of an enemy that had secured possession of the St. Lawrence Valley or Bermuda or the Gulf of Mexico. Short of this, an invasion of the eastern shores would be an attempted knock-out blow justifying the enormous risk involved. No blow limited to the Atlantic Coast of the United States could, I imagine, be decisive.

The real problem of invading the U.S. from the Atlantic Coast would be, how to force the line of the Alleghenies? The abundance of railroads and highways simplify but do not solve the problem.

There are three natural routes, no one of them particularly easy. The northernmost is the time-honored Hudson-Mohawk Valley following the New York Central Railroad. The southernmost—six hundred miles away—is the Potomac Valley and Cumberland Gap, now travelled by the Baltimore and Ohio Railroad. Between is the third and perhaps easiest route from the head of Chesapeake Bay up the Valley of the Susquehanna.

Of these three, the northernmost seems the most difficult. The Hudson River Valley is really an estuary in what was once a canyon. This canyon extends under water right out into the Atlantic where, at a point about 150 miles beyond Ambrose Light, its channel—already fifteen hundred feet below the "normal" ocean bed— "falls in tumult to a lifeless ocean."

This canyon can be defended at the Narrows, at the Palisades and elsewhere. It is a natural stronghold. The Catskills, themselves the "folded floor of ancient tropic seas," are a fine place in which to lose an enemy—as Rip Van Winkle found out.

The middle route, the Susquehanna Valley, now followed by the Lehigh Valley Railroad, leads through the heart of the Pennsylvania anthracite and industrial zone. Though it is often not over a mile wide and follows elaborate meanders, it is virtually level and leads into the Finger Lakes region of Central New York State without ever having climbed to over a thousand feet above the sea.

The Potomac-Cumberland Gap route in the south via Washington and the Baltimore and Ohio right of way would seem impassable if defended with passion—and adequate equipment.

Yet the best advice to a superior officer intent on piercing the Alleghenies, would be to go around them—to the north or south.

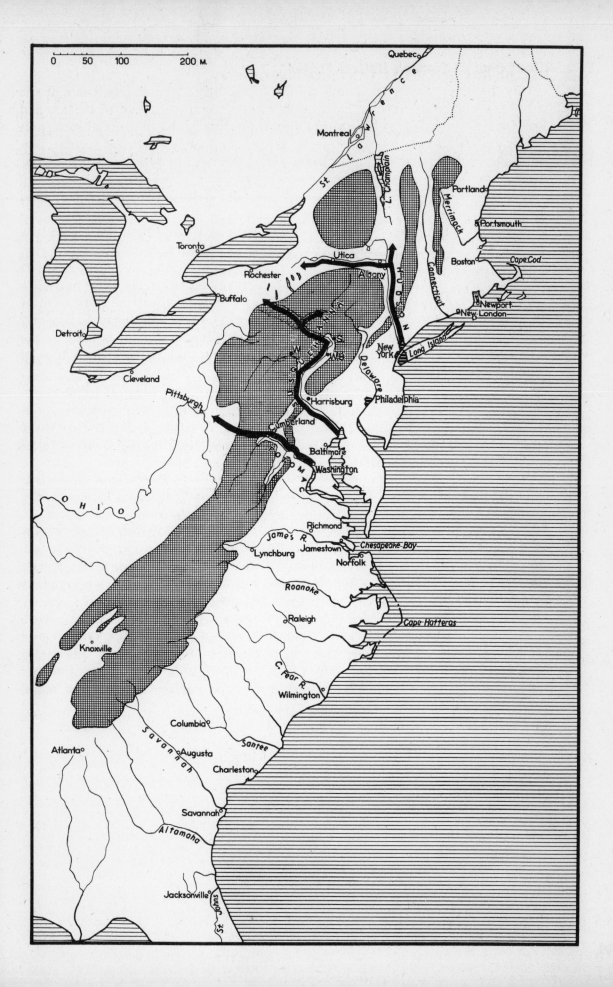

4. Hudson Bay and the St. Lawrence River Valley

Air power has made this region into the easiest invasion route of North America. From Berlin to Detroit, Michigan, there is not a single airplane hop of more than 900 statute miles and most are far shorter. Once you get to Greenland, establish yourself on the hospitable western side and create supply stores, you can move on into Hudson Bay. From Churchill and Moosonee on Hudson Bay, railroads bring you down to habitable Canada with the upper Mississippi Valley open before you. At the same time you might invade the St. Lawrence Valley. At least until recently. Until 1941 Labrador was one of the most desolate and militarily neglected areas on earth. But by the Spring of 1942 it had undergone a change. Combined Canadian and American forces were establishing series of air bases located strategically for both offensive and defensive war. The invitation to Axis parachutists to move without detection into this desert area and themselves establish the necessary fields for bases as springboards for further advances ceased to be.

The United Nations were not advertising the sites of these bases and it looked as though they might remain unknown until detected by the Axis or until the end of the war. Their creation completed the chain stretching up into Greenland and Iceland—a chain that could serve as well for reinforcing and invading Northern Europe as, in case events went the other way, for an Axis attempt on invading the United States. In this latter case, possible invasion lines into the United States might be Montreal-Boston or Moosonee-Detroit and Buffalo. An attempt to take the base at St. John's, Newfoundland, would seem indicated. But St. John's is still many hundred miles from the eastern industrial districts of the United States.

It should be apparent to anyone who gives thought to these maps that direct invasion of the United States by other than surprise attack offers such serious difficulties that only an extremely rash invader would undertake it.

Far more likely would be the following: an Axis that had driven the Americans out of Europe and Asia might, whether it entirely controlled the seas or not, be able to achieve and maintain air superiority. With such superiority alone it might take Alaska, the Panama Canal, the Caribbean area and Greenland. From these points it could start a ruthless air bombardment of the United States, concentrating on the murder of civilians and the terrorizing of the American people. Imagine a daily bombardment by a couple of thousand bombers accompanied by long-range battle-planes that could match American fighters and greatly outnumber them. Aluminum and copper stocks would run low, chromium and manganese and magnesium soon would be lacking. There would be none but artificial rubber—if plants for manufacture could be maintained under the hammering.

How long could resistance be maintained?

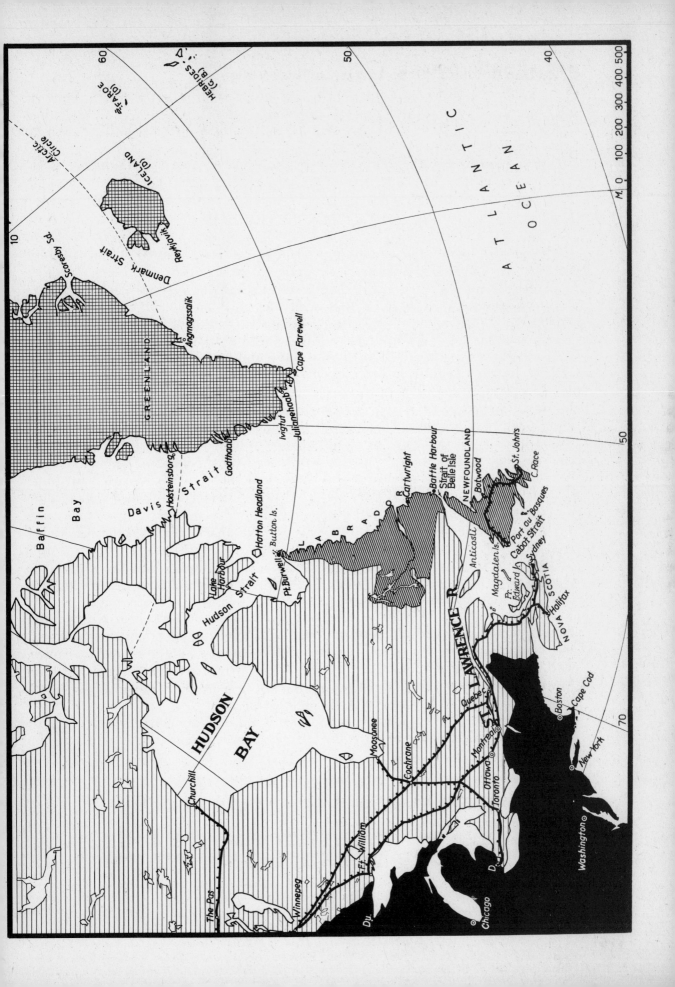

THE ATLANTIC OCEANS

The Atlantic Oceans are not very large as oceans go. But they are the most important on earth. Eighty percent of the world's sea-borne traffic in normal times follows these waters. Facing the Atlantic are located—with two or three exceptions—the richest and most powerful nations.

In the North Atlantic, industrial countries face each other; in the south, Africa and South America, both greatly productive of raw materials. The two Atlantics, the North and the South, are in shape roughly similar. From Greenland to Norway is about a thousand statute miles. At its widest, from Miami to Gibraltar, the North Atlantic, measures about 4500 statute miles. Where the North Atlantic meets the South Atlantic, the width (Natal to Freetown) is some 1850 statute miles. From Capetown to Montevideo is 4150 statute miles.

From the Atlantics there are but five water exits: into the Arctic; into the Pacific via the Caribbean and the Panama Canal; through Gibraltar Strait and the Great Inland Waterway to the Indian Ocean; around Africa into the Indian Ocean; around South America (or through Magellan Strait) into the Pacific.

In the struggle between the United Nations and Free French (white on this map) against the Axis (shown with occupied territories in black), with Portugal, Spain and Vichy France "neutral" (various degrees of shading), it soon appeared that Global Warfare required navies five to ten times as great as ever before, if the sea-lanes were to be made safe for the countries that nominally controlled the seas. Such navies would have to be protected by unimagined numbers of aircraft. While Axis submarines came and went freely almost anywhere in the Atlantics (subject to frequent but far from inevitable sinkings), Axis planes operating from Norway jeopardized the Arctic route to Soviet Russia, and Axis planes operating from Brittany played havoc with ships approaching Britain.

Dominating both Atlantics is the African bulge. Even after eliminating France, Axis forces dared not take over this area until they had also eliminated Soviet Russia, preferring to keep out British forces by leaving it in "neutral" Vichy French keeping. Once Russia were liquidated, Hitler might move in with his full forces through friendly Spain and helpless Portugal.

For air power, the key Atlantic area is Spanish Rio de Oro. French Dakar and British Sierra Leone and independent Liberia lie too far south; the Azores, Canaries and Madeira are too far north. But from Villa Cisneros in Rio de Oro, airplanes with a 2600 mile radius might patrol the Atlantics from Natal in Brazil to St. John's, Newfoundland, discovering if not preventing virtually all important troop or supply convoys between the United States and Europe or Africa.

Contrariwise, United Nations possession of the African bulge could make the opening and maintenance of a second European front against the Axis far less discouraging.

Sea Distances In Nautical Miles—1 nautical mile is equal to 1.15155 statute miles

Reykjavik	—	Faroes Is.	600	New York	— Murmansk	4319	New York — Rio de Janeiro	4770
Faroes Is.	—	North Scotland	320	New York	— Capetown	6786	New York — Buenos Aires	5871
New York	—	Port of Spain	1939	Capetown	— Freetown	3164	New York — Freetown	3757
				Capetown	— Rio de Janeiro	3273		

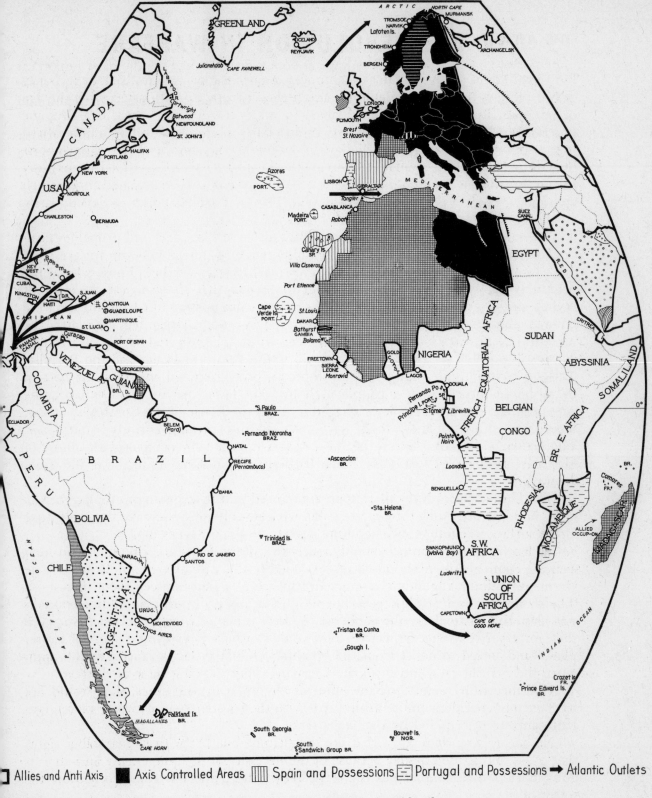

Allies and Anti Axis	Axis Controlled Areas	Spain and Possessions
Portugal and Possessions	Atlantic Outlets	

Air Distances in Statute Miles—1 statute mile is equal to 0.8684 nautical miles

New York	— Cape Farewell	1850	San Juan	— Panama Canal	1115	Miami	— Trinidad	1650
Cape Farewell	— Reykjavik	760	San Juan	— Port of Spain	620	Trinidad	— Belem (Para)	1302
Reykjavik	— Scapa Flow	715	New York	— Lisbon	3370	Belem (Para)	— Natal	925
Reykjavik	— Faroes Is.	595	New York	— Bermuda	775	Natal	— Freetown	1862
Reykjavik	— Bergen	905	Bermuda	— Azores	2065	Natal	— Rio de Janeiro	1436
New York	— Halifax	682	Azores	— Lisbon	1059	Rio de Janeiro	— Freetown	2965
Halifax	— St. John's	570	Lisbon	— Madeira	612	Rio de Janeiro	— Capetown	3765
St. John's	— Foynes	1925	Madeira	— Canary Is.	320	Rio de Janeiro	— Buenos Aires	1403
Halifax	— Cartwright	700	Canary Is.	— Cape Verde Is.	1002	Buenos Aires	— St. of Magellan	1618
Cartwright	— Julianehaab	600	Cape Verde Is.	— Dakar	475	St. of Magellan	— Capetown	4260
New York	— San Juan	1605	New York	— Miami	1075			

IV. THE REVOLUTION IN WARFARE

For thousands of years, human armies moved about on foot, or horseback or in horse-drawn vehicles, and forty miles a day was a good coverage. This lasted until the age of railroads. Even so trains are restricted to tracks. Laying new track is a tiresome process. World War One saw the first timid efforts at motorization as immortalized in the taxicab offensive of General Gallieni on the Marne and the Ourcq. For the first time, in 1917 I believe, airplanes extended their field from scouting, directing artillery fire and small-scale bombing to direct attacks upon troops. I participated in one such attack in 1918. It was not until World War Two that armies began to depend principally upon motorized wheels (tanks) and air power.

The same way with ships—from oars and sails to paddlewheel and propeller, coal-burning engines, oil-burning engines, gasoline engines—but always the surface ship, more heavily plated, shooting ever heavier projectiles even farther. Those who at the beginning of World War Two ventured to predict that the heaviest ships might become nothing but floating coffins unless protected against assault from the air were ignored, abused, derided—anything but believed. As late as December 1941, after the successful British attack upon the Italian Fleet within the protected harbor of Taranto, it was still possible for two great British ships, the Prince of Wales and the Repulse, fearlessly to steam into a danger zone without air protection and be sent to the bottom by air-borne torpedoes in a couple of hours. Yet less than five months later, the American and the Japanese fleets slugged it out at the Battle of the Coral Sea without shooting anything but anti-aircraft salvos; the fighting was done entirely by airplanes. The similar Battle of Midway Island, about a month later confirmed the snort of Major Al Williams: "Just what has a battleship ever done in this war but sink, anyway?"

The United States Navy thereupon announced that it was going to replace battleships, building or planned, by carriers. Yet what was obviously at stake was the future of the surface warship as such—and not merely of certain types of it.

Such a transformation occurs only rarely in history. Certain individuals had foreseen the coming supremacy of air power, notably the Italian General Douhet. The Germans, with their brand-new, younger armed forces, had foreseen more than most. Their use of air-borne troops, parachutists, gliders and transport planes, dive bombers was masterly; particularly the conquest of Crete remains a tactical classic. But even they got it partly wrong. Otherwise they would not have been caught short of fighter planes and forced to desist from the bombing of British cities exactly at the point when the British, unbeknown to the Germans, were showing signs of distress.

Had they fully understood the effect of air power against ships, they would not have encumbered their limited ship yards with the construction of two or more giant battleships to be crippled by airplane attack.

No one apparently foresaw that not the altitude bomber with its marvelous sights that could not be used by day because of the necessity of dodging enemy anti-aircraft guns; not the dive bomber but the torpedo-carrying plane was going to become the terror of the seas.

And still—on land and on sea—there was no end of technical developments in sight. A new weapon like an unsinkable battleship might reverse the entire trend. Effective development of radio-controlled planes and torpedo gliders could make it irresistible.

Airplanes (plus motor train vehicles) brought about yet another transformation of a type equally distressing and incomprehensible to conservatives: it widened the battle area to include the entire planet. It made war potentially global. Already World War One had gone some distance in this direction but the fact that one belligerent, the Central Powers, early lost their remote holdings, was an obstacle to the complete spread of hostilities, though naval battles occurred at a remote spot off the Falkland Islands and in the Indian Ocean. Even in 1942 a final obstacle to complete globality remained—aircraft were not yet sufficiently far ranging so that the Atlantic and Pacific ends of the Axis could keep in touch across the vastness of Soviet Russia. But the trend was manifest.

In this war, the United Nations were themselves spread far and wide. United Nations communications spanned the planet, United Nations forces, training or actually operating, were in more than twenty places. The simple geography of the new war put a severe strain on even the most cultured minds. But for their potentially superior resources, the United Nations would have been unable to stand against Axis forces operating on (generally) inside lines.

A third military transformation was inherent in the development of democracy: psychological warfare. When leaders were a small close group, propaganda could usually accomplish little. But against a mass of citizens often more literate than educated, it proved possible to direct a stream of intellectual missiles—to plan and carry out wars of nerves, to divide and conquer populations, to mislead the impressionable, and to mobilize the self-seeking and the traitorous against their own governments. This sort of thing culminated in Hitler's capture of Austria by a visit from Schuschnigg; of Czechoslovakia by a fierce speech and ultimatum; in Japan's successful blackmail of the United States State Department—Give me oil and scrap iron or I shall attack the Dutch Indies!—thus acquiring the supplies with which they ultimately attacked the Dutch Indies. In World War One this new weapon was moderately but effectively wielded by the Allies; in the non-violent phase of World War Two, and up to 1942, the United Nations were far outdone by the Axis. It was curious: democratic leaders whose political and commercial structures had largely been propped on posters, slogans, selling talks, were hesitant to believe that such devices could be effective against Germans, Italians and Japanese. Yet so obvious were the effects of psychological warfare when waged by the Axis, that no modern commander could entirely dispense with it.

The development of new weapons and techniques, the spread of combat over the entire planet, the emergence of psychological warfare—these three combined to bring about a complete revolution in strategy.

In the understanding and utilization of the revolutionary possibility, the best military minds followed—no doubt, inevitably followed—one jump behind the events. Readers of this Atlas will almost surely have noticed uncertainty in the writer's own

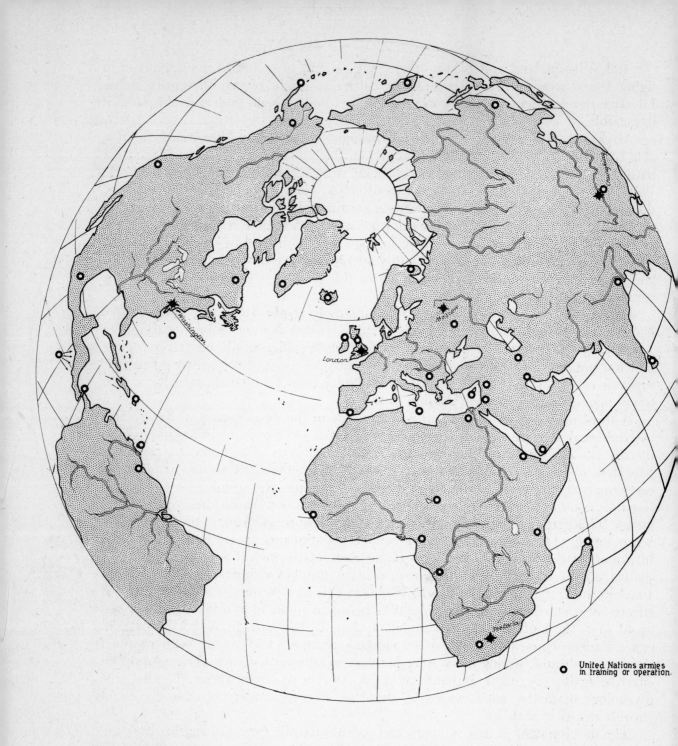

United Nations armies
in training or operation.

conceptions and how, from text to text, he seems to wobble. On one page he writes of winning by "gittin' there fu'stest with the mostest imagination" and then reverts to common and classical conceptions of land and sea warfare—almost as though these things had not changed since the days of Julius Caesar. The explanation is that the writer simply does not know how much of classical strategy will be left when present possibilities are coherently worked out. His excuse is that the commanders in the present struggle—to judge by their trial-and-error methods—do not feel very sure

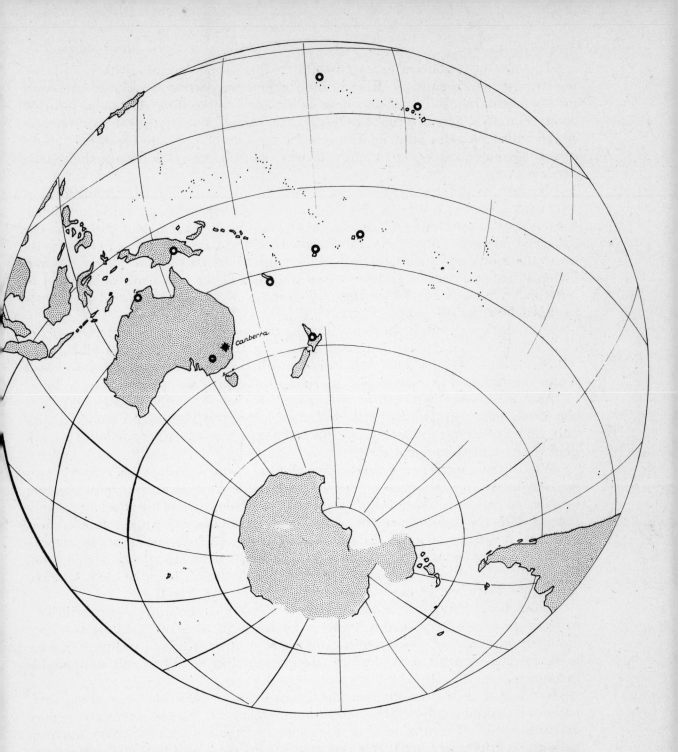

about it themselves. In one area United Nations forces have been pushed back three times in almost identical manner by an enemy possessing virtually the same superior equipment: the German 88 millimeter all-purpose gun had in the Battles of Flanders and of France in 1940 shown itself supreme. There was no wild scramble on the part of United Nations leaders to imitate or surpass it. Numerous newspapermen foresaw just about what happened in Malaya, Burma and the Dutch Indies—and were ignored by the experts.

The current revolution in warfare—this at least seems certain—is likely to prove the strongest single political factor in the contemporary world. Sooner or later—and for the sake of humanity one may hope as soon as possible—it seems bound to bring about a totally different form of political organization. For strategical requirements are becoming such that only the strongest and most developed nations—or federations of smaller ones—can hope to wield sufficient political power to protect their independence.

Experts may differ as to minor requirements, but the chief one is a giant force of aircraft. These may well be of the following kinds: short-range pursuits; long-range fighters capable of crossing the smaller oceans and the larger seas, and returning; far-flying reconnaissance planes; several types of bombers; torpedo planes of one or more sorts; transports and freight planes, gliders and glider-tankers for longer distance flying. Whether aircraft will have driven warships off the seas is distinctly open to question; if not, then many of these types may have to be duplicated in slightly modified form for use from carriers.

Since ships may still be necessary for the transporting of heavy materials—if not men—overseas, then submarines operating against freighters on the vast global runs will enjoy such an advantage that to cope with their danger, war fleets of vessels ten or twenty times as numerous as anything that exists today will have to be built.

And in addition there will be the demand for motor transport and tanks for a completely motorized land-army, with various new sorts of tanks and mounted anti-tank guns, ever newer and more powerful and more accurate artillery and anti-aircraft guns; heavier machine guns, etc.

With such weapons in the hands of a potential enemy, a vulnerable country must not only match its strength in immediately utilizable equipment, but must garrison heavily and permanently all its important centers within reach of air attack (a distance varying with the improvement of planes), thus maintaining a huge standing army and navy; it will also be compelled to construct a host of subterranean supply factories completely impervious to air attack, equipped much like the unfortunate Maginot Line. Other industries will have to be so scattered that they cannot be easily knocked out—to the detriment of peacetime efficiency.

In other words, not only a fair percentage of every nation's man-power will have to be more or less permanently under arms, with all sorts of plans for two-hour mobilization in case of attack, but a giant segment of the national income will have to be invested in what men of saner times would feel bound to call unprofitable investment.

Nor is this all. Let us suppose that peoples can be persuaded to ransom their national independence by the permanent impoverishment. Even so, only a few regions on earth would seem capable of creating and maintaining such super-armament as national security might need. Few countries possess the requisite skilled man-power, the requisite raw materials—steel, aluminum, manganese, nickel, petroleum (or coal): the United States, Great Britain (if control of the seas can be maintained); Germany (with France, Luxemburg, Belgium); Soviet Russia—and only many years hence—China and India, perhaps. Countries incapable of such construction and maintenance would, under the present system, be destined to dependence or worse. Yet the burdens on the ruling peoples would be such as to make the lot of these dependents almost enviable.

Impossible? Certainly not. Fantastic? Admitted. Yet this forecast is only a projection into the future, on the basis of the maintenance of the present International System of fully sovereign National States, of tendencies admittedly dominant in June 1942.

If these tendencies make the future lurid as a dyspeptic's dream, that is not the writer's fault.

But is there a conceivable alternate? Perhaps. Global Wars in an ever accelerating series can be staved off only by the organization of Global Peace. This is the sort of peace that the partisans of the old League of Nations instinctively felt must be sought. A Global Peace is an indivisible peace—a peace that is maintained everywhere on the planet by superior force, if necessary at the cost of some fighting. Call this fighting war, or call it police action, it is at present the only practical substitute for thorough-going, oppressive militarism. Since no single Power is at present capable of exercising supremacy over the planet, once Germany's second attempt be thwarted, it follows that police surveillance must be exercised either by a permanently predominant alliance of Sovereign States, or by an international body. A permanent alliance —U.S.A., British Commonwealth, Soviet Russia, perhaps a resuscitated France and Poland, China—could do the trick all right. But it could not be maintained. To be permanent, an Alliance must have a dangerous adversary. When two or more Sovereign States combine, it is always *against* someone, never *for* something. Remove the danger and the alliance disintegrates. What remains degenerates with mathematical certainty into a Balance of Power, to compose which any other country, even yesterday's mortal enemy, is not too hated to be admitted. Result: the Armed Sovereign State system re-emerges, with its attributes, militarism, and wars. The only hope, therefore, lies in policing by a sovereign international body.

How this can and should be accomplished –a revival of the League, a development of the present United Nations, some form of Union Now, something as yet un-dreamed of, the present writer does not know. He does not know that it will be accom-plished, or even tried. But with the ancient fatal chain—crushing militarism, new alliances, new wars—lurking so darkly upon a none-too-distant horizon, with the casual nexus between past isolationism and World War Two so shriekingly obvious, he dares to hope that the fundamental common sense that kept mankind alive for so many thousands of years will not fail us now.

INDEX

Talinn, 14
Thailand, 17, 30
Third Reich, 9
Three-Ocean Powers, 9
Tierra del Fuego, 44
Timor Strait, 54, 55
Topography, security values of, 25
Toronto, 75, 116
Torres Strait, 52, 53, 54
Trans-Siberian Railway, 65, 68
Trinidad, 39, 40, 42
Turkestan-Siberian Railway, 65, 68
Two-ocean powers in 1939, 9

Ukraine, 30
Umano, cited on elements of power, 26, 28
Union of Soviet Socialist Republics, 9, 10, 24; area of influence, 14-15; manpower, 26; wheat exports, 30; Arctic areas developed by, 50; railways, 68, 69

United Kingdom. *See* Great Britain.
United Nations, industrial strength, 28; wheat exports, 30
United States of America, 9, 24; balanced power in, 10-12; area of influence map, 13; wheat exports, 30; gold reserves, 33; units of income, 34, 35; railway development, 74, 75; invasion routes: West Coast, 110, 111; Mississippi Valley, 112, 113; Eastern section, 114, 115; Hudson Bay and St. Lawrence Valley, 116, 117; Atlantic Ocean, 118, 119
Ushuaia, 44

Varangers, route of, 92, 93
Venezuela, 42
Vichy France. *See* France.
Vladivostok, 14, 16, 48, 51, 105, 107, 109

3

Wake Island, 12, 107, 109
War engines, distance factors, 25
Warfare, revolution in, 120 ff.; ship development, 120; air-power development, 120-121; psychological, 121-124; future possibilities, 124-126
Washington, 13, 115, 117
Waterways communication, 36-63; all-ocean sea lanes, 36-38; Caribbean Sea area, 38-40; Panama Canal, 40; inland, 40-41, 60-63; Indian Ocean, 56-57. *See also* Sea routes.
Wealth, form of, 28. *See also* Income.
West Indies, 38-43
Wheat production, 30, 31
Wickard, Claude, quoted on food importance, 30
Windward Islands, 38
Windward Passage, 40
Wirth, Hermann, quoted on origin of Nordics, 50
Wood, Junius, cited on Soviet territory, 14